A guide for soul friends

The art of the spiritual companion

Ray Simpson

and members of the
Community of Aidan and Hilda

kevin mayhew

kevin
mayhew

First published in Great Britain in 2008 by Kevin Mayhew Ltd
Buxhall, Stowmarket, Suffolk IP14 3BW
Tel: +44 (0) 1449 737978 Fax: +44 (0) 1449 737834
E-mail: info@kevinmayhewltd.com

www.kevinmayhew.com

9 8 7 6 5 4 3 2 1 0

ISBN 978 1 84867 073 0
Catalogue No. 1501132

Cover design by Rob Mortonson
Edited by Katherine Laidler
Typeset by Richard Weaver

Printed and bound in Great Britain

Contents

Ray Simpson is an Anglican priest and the guardian of the Community of Aidan and Hilda, a dispersed community with a retreat house on Holy Island. He is the author of numerous bestselling books on Celtic spirituality.

This book draws from several previously published sources: my books *Soul Friendship: Celtic insights into spiritual mentoring* (Hodder & Stoughton, 1999) and *Celtic Spirituality: Rhythm, roots and relationship* (Grove, 2003); and *A Beginner's Guide for Soul Friends and Those They Accompany* (St Aidan Press, 2007), written by a working party of the Community of Aidan and Hilda. Members included Graham and Ruth Booth, Carol Few, Gary Hemmings, Heather Macdonald, Liz Toy and myself. I am grateful for the working party's permission to use this material.

To keep it simple we use the term *soul friend* for the person who offers guidance and the term *seeker* for the person who seeks it.

Introduction

Why there's a global hunger for the soul friend

In our 24/7 society everything is mass-produced – food, internet, advertising. This leaves out our need for individuality.

Data overload, choice fatigue, celebrity culture, fast living and excess noise distract us from attending to our inner life.

In our global, mobile planet, family and community bonds weaken. People cry out for authentic one-to-one friendship, for help to find their true path – for a soul friend.

The twenty-first century has seen a massive spread of:

Life coaches

These help you succeed in your goals – for example, improved income, fitness, relationships or stress management. However, if your ego is setting your goals, a life coach merely helps you to live a selfish life more effectively.

Mentors

In business and youth enablement programmes, mentors – people who help trainees understand the ethos of the organisation and how to achieve its goals effectively – are widely used. They may not, however, help trainees to discover their true self, develop a relationship with God, or relate their work to the wider well-being of the world.

Soulmates

Entire pages of some newspapers and internet sites are filled with advertisements for a soulmate. Soulmates, however, may simply be two lonely people holding hands as they sink.

For such reasons there is a global search for a different kind of enabler. This enabler is a true friend. A true friend wants the best for the real me, and has the insight to know that my highest good lies in finding and following God's will. Different countries and cultures have different names for such a person.

Catholics and others use the term *spiritual director*. If he is a priest, they may confess their sins to him. Orthodox Christians in Russia value the *staretz* – a holy hermit who has deep spiritual understanding. Today many evangelical Christians are reviving this practice. People who offer such guidance may be called *whole life disciplers*, *sacred companions*, or *spiritual guides*. In Norway they are discovering the *medvandrer* – a person who walks with you on your life journey, slowly, at your own pace. Early Christians in Ireland met with the *anam cara*. This Irish term, which has recently become popular in many nations and languages, translates into English as *soul friend*. The Irish taught that a person without a soul friend was like a human body without a head.

Bible examples

The Bible has many examples of such people: Deborah and Huldah (both prophetesses); Jonathan and David (who became Israel's great king); Elizabeth and Mary (the mothers of John the Baptist and Jesus); the apostle Paul and his young helper, Timothy. Even then they had the problem that too few Christians had experience of this art: 'You have many teachers but few of you are spiritual parents,' wrote the apostle Paul.

The supreme example of the soul friend is Jesus, who spent three years discipling twelve people.

Often soul friends have some professional training or have emerged from a religious or solitary calling which involves constant reflection. Unfortunately, far more people seek a soul friend than there are available, and some find the relationship too impersonal or intimidating. Now there are moves to professionalise soul friends further, partly because of concerns about abuse or litigation. Thus in some spheres only those who have done certain courses and are on an approved list are recognised as soul friends.

Many people who are looking for a soul friend are willing to start with someone they can trust who shares their own desire to journey with God and who is willing to learn from mistakes even as they accompany them.

I am Guardian of the dispersed international Community of Aidan and Hilda and I live on the Holy Island of Lindisfarne near Berwick-upon-Tweed. King Oswald of England decreed that Lindisfarne should be called holy because Bishop Aidan's seventh-century mission to the English and Celts was based there.

Our Community invites people to journey with God, and to keep before us ten waymarks which help us not to stray. We meet with a soul friend to talk through how we may apply these common waymarks to our own unique circumstances and temperament. We now have fifteen years' experience of this practice, with its possibilities and pitfalls.

At first we strove towards each member having a trained and accredited soul friend. However, this left too many people stranded without the right soul friend. Often members were unable to find a soul friend in their area. Those members who found a soul friend sometimes found their approach unsuited to their particular needs. We needed soul friends who were sufficiently flexible to use whatever tools would best support the member's faith journey, and who were willing to be regarded as a friend.

Now, in certain cases, a Voyager in our Community (that is, a mature Christian who commits to follow the Way of Life) spends time praying and working through with another Voyager how best to apply the Way of Life to their present circumstances. These we sometimes call Companions on the Way. Increasingly churches desire their members to meet in twos to mentor one another.

To avoid the lowering of standards and traps that befall the inexperienced, those who aspire to be a soul friend need to:

- foster the habit of daily reflection
- walk closely with God
- spend time in prayer
- develop listening skills

It may be helpful to keep the image of an escalator before us. The giants among soul friends may be steps ahead of someone who accompanies a friend for the first time, but, through reflection, listening and prayer, everyone may advance.

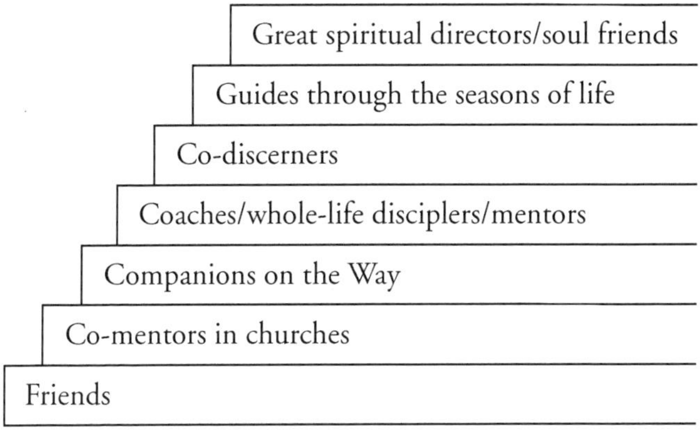

The soul friendship escalator

This guide book is especially for those who have newly stepped on to the escalator. It answers frequently asked questions and explores ways a friend may accompany another. It gradually ascends the escalator, ending at the top with glimpses of some of the world's greatest spiritual guides.

The great spiritual guides from the Desert Fathers, the Celtic Church and more recent times have inspired the Church for many generations and beckon us to follow in their footsteps. For, wherever we are on the escalator, our common desire is surely to see the seeker evolve into 'God's work of art' (Ephesians 2:10).

CHAPTER 1

Things to know before you start

What is a soul friend?

A soul friend helps another person, in one-to-one meetings, to:

- grow in their relationship with God and others
- explore different ways of praying
- reflect on the inner promptings of the Holy Spirit
- feed on Scripture
- gain self-awareness
- find comfort and strength in times of adversity
- develop their potential as a human being created in the image of God
- apply the Gospel to each area of their life – for example, money, sex, work
- maintain a good balance of prayer, work and recreation
- identify how God has led them in the past, reflect on where they are now and discern direction for the future

What sort of person should be a soul friend?

A person who:

- walks closely with God
- has experience of life and faith
- understands the steps of the spiritual journey

- has a deep knowledge of Scripture
- can explore different ways of praying and learning
- understands people and is able to build a trusting relationship
- listens attentively with humility
- is non-judgemental
- has a high regard for confidentiality
- offers unconditional acceptance
- is willing to challenge
- refrains from giving advice and setting their own agenda
- has knowledge of resources and books on Christian formation

Can two people be soul friends to one another?

It is possible for two mature Christians to be mutual soul friends. However, there is a danger of becoming too emotionally involved. Boundaries need to be defined and confidentiality maintained. Both people need to be supported by their church community and safeguards put in place.

Should a soul friend be directive or non-directive?

New Christians need teaching on the fundamentals of the Christian faith, advice on how to pray, read the Bible, and follow some form of community Way of Life. For example, in its Way of Life, the Community of Aidan and Hilda recognises the value of prophecy in the ministry of soul friendship. However, as people mature in their faith, the relationship between the soul friend and the seeker changes and becomes much less directive.

Attentive listening and the ability to facilitate the seeker to hear directly from God is the basis of the ministry of soul friendship. During prayer, a picture, a word, or insight might come to mind for the seeker. This may give the soul friend insight into how to explore a new way forward for the seeker. However, rather than tell the seeker directly, it is wiser to explore this insight and facilitate the seeker in a process of self-discovery.

Do soul friends have to be accredited or approved?

New vocations to the ministry of soul friendship are emerging among the people of God. To be a soul friend requires some training in spiritual direction or prayer guidance. Supervision is a valuable and necessary support for soul friends.

When new seekers choose a soul friend in the community of Aiden and Hilda, the soul friend needs to indicate that they are either an ordained minister, a member of a religious community or otherwise authorised by their church to be a soul friend.

Who convenes the meetings?

It is the seeker who contacts the soul friend to arrange the first meeting. It is wise to plan one introductory meeting to begin with. At the end of the first session the soul friend gives the seeker the opportunity to decide if they would like to arrange another meeting. However, the seeker may prefer to consider before making a decision. If the seeker wants to continue, two more sessions can be arranged. After these have taken place, there should be a review to discern whether the soul friend and the seeker both want to continue for a longer period. It is important that the seeker feels free to discontinue meeting without feeling under an obligation to continue.

How often and for how long should the soul friend and the seeker meet?

The frequency and duration should be what both find appropriate to their situation, and they may fluctuate. Two sessions each year are a minimum. Four 90-minute sessions per year are typical. If the soul friend and seeker live far apart, they may meet less often, spending a day or two in retreat together.

Suppose you mentor someone for the first time. How do you get to know their character, circumstances and spiritual journey?

These are some questions you could ask:

- What is your heart's longing?
- What are your passions and interests?
- What are your strengths?
- What are your weaknesses?
- What is your family/school/work situation?
- What are your talents?
- What are your dreams?

- What do you most want to learn?
- What question do you most want to ask me?
- What do you want to achieve through our meetings?
- What do you want us to do during these meetings?

You could ask the seeker to make a life-line:

The seeker draws a straight line on a blank sheet of paper. The seeker writes 'birth' at the start of this line and 'now' at the end.

Ask the seeker to make up to five marks on this line to represent the key moments of change, challenge or encounter with God.

Birth Now

Can you describe some different approaches in soul friendship?

Here are five examples.

1. Teaching

The soul friend helps the seeker find balance and rhythm in daily life and develop strategies for achieving goals, overcoming obstacles, healing relationships and learning the faith.

2. Listening to God and to each other

Attentive listening is the foundation of the soul friendship relationship.

Dependency on the Holy Spirit enables the ministry of inner healing and the discernment of the will of God.

3. Gospel meditation and discernment

This approach is based on the ideas of St Ignatius of Loyola, founder of the Society of Jesus and best known for his *Spiritual Exercises* (see also page 65 ff.).

During Gospel meditation seekers visualise themselves with Jesus in episodes from the Gospels. They meditate on what they can see, hear and feel as they imagine they are participating in the story. Close encounter with Jesus in the imagination of our own hearts enables life-changing self-awareness and inner transformation.

Discernment begins with becoming aware of different moods and feelings which are either life-giving, leading us towards God, or deadening, leading us away from God. Acknowledging the reality of our feelings and inner promptings of the Holy Spirit enables us to make objective decisions and life choices.

4. Contemplation

During the session the soul friend and the seeker might agree to spend time being still before God. In the silence, thoughts and feelings rise to the surface, revealing issues that are important.

5. Coaching for spiritual fitness

The early Desert Fathers focused on the path of spiritual discipline and detachment from the world. In their quest for holiness they sought to enable those who came to them for guidance to gain self-awareness of destructive thought patterns and motivation, and replace them with truthful perceptions and life-giving decisions and choices – for example, replacing destructive passions with their opposite virtues.

Other questions

What is holistic spiritual direction?

In order to realise our full humanity we need to understand our life as a whole, including both the past and the present. Once the jigsaw of our life is known, the shapes resolve into a pattern, and our relationship with self, God and others can be whole.

Holistic means that a person relates to the world as a whole, rather than to fragments of it as ends in themselves. A soul friend will therefore explore prayerfully with a seeker different life areas – for example, money, work, sex, home, relationships, involvement in the community and responsibilities for the environment.

What does it mean to be accountable?

Once trust has been established a seeker need hold nothing back from the soul-friend. The seeker may give account of their use of time, talent, money, opportunity, power and sex; of their handling of weaknesses and their relationships in home, work, church and society. Trust grows in its own time. Transparent sharing of the heart cannot be hurried but neither should it be unduly held back.

Can the soul friend and seeker keep in contact in other ways?

It is advisable for a seeker to choose a soul friend who is not a member of their own church because objectivity is important in the soul friend relationship. Contact needs to be planned and boundaries need to be clear. However, this will depend on individual circumstances.

How does the seeker prepare for meeting with the soul friend?

Keeping a prayer journal and writing down matters as they

arise helps to focus on the most important issues to bring to the session.

How does a soul friend prepare for meeting with the seeker?

Before agreeing to take on a seeker, a soul friend needs to be sure that they have time to meet regularly.

- Allow time to prepare in prayer before the seeker arrives
- Pray regularly for the seeker between sessions

Should a soul friend be consulted before making life choices?

It is wise for a seeker to consult their soul friend before making major life-changing decisions.

Exercises

For individual or group reflection

1. Reflect on a person known to you who you think has the gifts and qualities needed to be a soul friend and write them down. Add to the list other qualities that you would be looking for in a soul friend.

2. Read the story of Jesus' encounter with the Samaritan woman in John 4:4-30.

   Imagine yourself in the place of the Samaritan woman as she meets Jesus sitting by the well. Spend time listening to him.

   What are the gifts and qualities that you recognise in him as you talk together?

   Make a few notes on your reflections.

CHAPTER 2

Friends: getting started

Building a relationship

Establishing a relationship of trust and openness is the foundation of the soul-friendship ministry.

The first session

- Pray
- Prepare a space to meet that is comfortable and free of interruptions
- Informal welcome
- Share what seems important and might be relevant from your own life story
- Explore with the seeker their hopes and expectations for the session
- Give a simple overview of your understanding of soul friendship
- Inform them if you have a supervisor and explain briefly
- Assure them of confidentiality at all times, except when the seeker or someone else's well-being is at risk
- Ask them if they would like to consider coming for another session
- If you feel somebody else would be more suitable to meet the seeker's needs, suggest making a referral

What format might a soul-friend session take?

The format should be attuned to the needs of the seeker and unfolds in response to the leading of the Holy Spirit. However, a simple structure, which can be adapted as the need arises, gives a sense of direction and meaning to the session.

For example:

- Welcome
- Review of events and experience since the last session
- Brief time of prayer
- Take time to discover what the seeker most wants to talk about
- Attentive listening – tune in to thoughts, feelings and motivations
- Reflect back to the person what has been expressed, to establish empathy and mutual understanding
- Consider the issue in relation to the ten elements of the Way of Life. These are:
  - life-long learning
  - spiritual journey
  - rhythm of prayer, work and recreation
  - spiritual initiatives through intercession
  - simple lifestyle
  - care of creation
  - healing fragmented people and communities
  - openness to God's Spirit
  - unity
  - mission

- Explore possible options for a way forward if appropriate
- Summarise what has occurred in the session
- Pray together
- During the session there may be times of prayer and reflection or reading from Scripture
- After the session has finished, agree a date for the next meeting

Should a soul friend make notes after the session?

Keeping a few notes after the session helps the soul friend to prepare prayerfully for the next session. It is important to ask the seeker's permission first. Notes should be kept under lock and key in a place to which no one else has access. When making notes, remember that the seeker may ask to see them.

Exercises

For individual or group reflection

1. Make an outline of a soul-friendship session, including aspects that you would find helpful if you were the seeker. Make another list of aspects you would find unhelpful. Take time to reflect on the differences.

2. Telling your story – it can be helpful for a seeker to gain self-awareness and discern the presence of God by writing their own autobiography from childhood to the present day.

They should note the times when they have experienced the presence of God.

In your own time write your own autobiography. Include the times when God has felt close by and when he has seemed to be far away.

Suggested reading

W. A. Barry and W. J. Connolly, *The Practice of Spiritual Direction* (Seabury, 1982). This is a practical book written by two priests with many years' experience in training Spiritual Directors at the Centre for Religious Development in Cambridge, Massachusetts, USA.

CHAPTER 3

Co-mentors in churches

How churches may develop faith journey companions

In the past, only a few churches encouraged their members to use a spiritual director. Some churches have felt that their members' needs for nurture and guidance can be met through sharing in cells or groups.

The Shepherd's Guidebook: Spiritual and Practical Foundations for Cell Group Leaders by Ralph W. Neighbour (Touch Outreach Ministries, 1996) includes useful lists of procedures for getting acquainted, developing an apprentice, taking the role of teacher, facilitator and coach. It suggests that these questions are asked during opening chit-chat to break the ice:

What is your . . .

- greatest regret?
- happiest moment?
- biggest weakness and strength?
- favourite place?
- hardest challenge?
- dream?
- fear?

Cells and groups, however, have their limits. Some of a person's deepest, most sensitive needs are not appropriate to share in a group, where not everyone can be guaranteed to respect confidentiality or have the insight and emotional space to respond appropriately.

Now, therefore, an increasing number of churches seek to encourage members to meet in twos and mentor one another. This, too, has its dangers, but these are lessened if the co-mentoring is within a supervisory framework which includes some input.

One way to establish co-mentoring is through a programme, such as the author's *The Transforming Church* (Kevin Mayhew, 2008) which provides log books for two people to discuss and fill in together. After this a pair could go through a book on spiritual disciplines. Adele Ahlberg Calhoun's *Spiritual Disciplines Handbook* (InterVarsity Press, 2005) and *The Christian Educator's Handbook of Spiritual Formation*, edited by Kenneth O. Gangel and James C. Wilhoit (Baker Books, 1998) are two examples.

Another way is to capitalise on the natural 'let's meet up for coffee' meetings which already exist between two church friends. Meeting with a friend can be like the refreshing pool mentioned in Psalm 23. The church leadership can suggest ways in which they may make more focused use of this time in order to build one another up.

If this idea seems strange, a church might introduce it as a six-week experiment in Lent. If enough people find this valuable, they may then continue it.

What to do at each meeting

Two friends who meet weekly, fortnightly or monthly may choose to allocate the first half of their coffee meeting to one person and the second half to the other. Or they may prefer to use the whole of one meeting for one person, and reverse roles at their next meeting.

Each friend in turn will begin by sharing how they carried out the suggestions made at their previous meeting.

After that they agree on their aims for the meeting, and the seeker shares something under each numbered heading. The soul friend listens, clarifies anything they do not understand, and reflects back what they think the seeker has said. Only then does the soul friend share any thought, Scripture or experience which may help the seeker, or they may suggest the seeker goes straight on to the next point.

Some may wish to pray together before they part, or the soul friend may offer to pray for the seeker at home.

Before you begin – how to think of yourselves

Think of your life as a journey. You are journeying towards:

- wholeness
- good relationships
- being in the right place and job at the right time
- increased knowledge and love of God and of God's world
- human fullness and creativity

You therefore need to leave behind wrong things that hold you back or stages of life that you have outgrown.

Here are suggestions for an initial four meetings:

First meeting: discerning where I am in my life journey

The Bible is packed with references to how God led people. Look some up – for example, how Abraham was guided to leave home (Genesis 12-25); how Isaac found a wife (Genesis 24); how Miriam saved her baby brother, Moses (Exodus 2:1-10).

The seeker:

- tells their soul friend the most significant events in each quarter of their life so far
- describes what they feel they have completed in life and can now leave behind
- shares their deepest unfulfilled aspiration for the future

Discuss together:

- what stage of life the seeker may have reached
- a relevant Bible passage to meditate on through the week
- any activity that may be appropriate
- any next step that may be taken

Second meeting: dealing with frustrations

- The seeker tells their soul friend what frustrates them most at the moment, and hinders them moving forward on their faith journey. The soul friend draws out whether this is a symptom of a deeper underlying frustration.
- The seeker discusses with the soul friend how much their frustration is the result of their selfish will being crossed, and how much it is the consequence of God's will for them being hindered. How do they know the difference?

- The soul friend points to a similar frustration experienced by someone in the Bible or by a living person, and discusses how that was dealt with. For example, if the problem is that the seeker is at everyone's beck and call, the soul friend could read about Jesus' similar problem in John 11:1-8.
- How did Jesus make up his mind to say 'no' to some requests and 'yes' to others? He evaluated them in the light of his priorities. Discuss what the seeker's priorities are.
- In the light of these priorities, what actions should the seeker take to deal with their frustrations?

Third meeting: overcoming weaknesses

We all have weaknesses. Perhaps we are addicted to a substance, habit or relationship. Perhaps we fail to do or be what we should. Perhaps we neglect to look after our body, mind, spirit or relationships.

Fitness programmes abound to help us overcome flabby bodies. They include exercise and diet. Early Christians developed fitness programmes to help overcome flabby souls (soul = body-mind-spirit). They were called athletes of the Spirit.

The two basic ideas are to master cravings by going without something we crave; and to undertake a spiritual exercise which increases in us the virtue which is the opposite of the vice.

The seeker tells the soul friend of the main weakness they wish to overcome at the present time, and they discuss ways of doing it.

Fourth meeting: healing

- The seeker thinks beforehand about hurts, fears or emotional responses which need healing, and shares with the soul friend the one that most needs healing.
- The soul friend discusses this, shares any insight, reads a helpful Bible passage, and prays for the seeker.
- After discussion, the soul friend suggests something the seeker will give up for an agreed period that will help them master their bad habit. This could be anything – excess food, drink, TV, car or shopping trips, talking, hiding away, casual sexual intercourse which betrays a committed relationship, late nights – you name it. If the weakness takes the form of taking it out on others, the soul friend might suggest a form of restitution.
- The soul friend then suggests an exercise that will help build the virtue that matches the vice.

  Here are a few examples:

  If the problem is greed or over-indulgence, it is good not only to give something up but also to give something to others – alms, presents or time.

  If the problem is taking it out on others or causing discord, it is good not only to give up the bad practice but also to make restitution by doing something for them or by making an act of unity.

  If the problem is slackness or neglect, it is good not only to cut things that waste time but also to prioritise duties and use some sleep or pleasure time to carry these out.

  If the problem is some form of pride, the exercise might be to do some good deed each day which is anonymous.

- The soul friend suggests a Scripture verse for the seeker to repeat frequently through the week or a passage on which to meditate, which builds up the needed virtue.

CHAPTER 4

Companions on the Way

A Way of Life with a soul friend

We have likened the diverse kinds of soul friend to people on an escalator (see page 9). People on the first step we sometimes name Companions on the Way. These may not be highly trained soul friends, but they are genuine, thoughtful friends, whom a seeker may trust and with whom the seeker may report, reflect and pray. Growing numbers now adopt a Rule or Way of Life, which they talk through with a friend. The framework of a dispersed community or a local church safeguards against a relationship that becomes inward-looking or lacks purpose.

Early Celtic soul friends lived within the framework of a Rule of Life which their community espoused or which they kept as wandering hermits or anchorites. Some of the lay seekers they befriended would be influenced by the Rule of their local monastic community. The fourteenth-century soul friend St Morgan writes:

> In a single day we make so many decisions we cannot possibly weigh up the good and evil consequences of each decision.
>
> We are liable to make foolish and wrong decisions. For this reason we need a rule, a simple set of moral principles that we can apply to each decision we make. This will not be foolproof, but with a good rule, our decision will far more often be right than wrong. (See also page 53 ff.)

A Way of Life sets out the values and goals of a community or an individual, and a checklist of practices which help them to live these.

New networks are emerging which draw Christians from diverse streams to commit themselves to some form of Rule.

This chapter illustrates this practice with the ten waymarks of the Community of Aidan and Hilda's Way of Life (see below), but others may adapt this to their own life patterns.

Once a year, before meeting with a soul friend, the seeker reflects on how they aim to apply each of the ten waymarks to their present circumstances. The seeker gives a written account to their soul friend. The soul friend and the seeker then explore the ten waymarks together. The soul friend helps the seeker to focus on important issues and plan steps that are realistic – for example, relationship with God, family, work, recreation and responsibilities in the local and global community. This may take more than one session.

A helpful companion is the commentary on the Way of Life by the author: *A Pilgrim Way: New Celtic monasticism for everyday people* (Kevin Mayhew, 2005).

The ten waymarks and suggestions for each

1. Life-long learning

- Enable the seeker to discover ways of entering into the presence of God revealed through creation, Scripture and life experience.

- Encourage the seeker to develop a reflective lifestyle and explore what can be learnt from their relationships with others, their personal circumstances and life events.

- Consider possible adjustments in attitudes and objectives needed, according to the seeker's present stage of life.
- Develop a plan of Bible study and other areas of learning.

Suggested reading

Ray Simpson, *Celtic Daily Light* (Kevin Mayhew, 2003), provides readings for every day of the year. It includes quotations from the writings of the Desert Fathers and Celtic Christians and tells stories about them.

Ray Simpson, *Exploring Celtic Spirituality* (Kevin Mayhew, 2004), provides a study guide.

More information can be found on the website www.aidanandhilda.org.uk

2. Spiritual journey

- The soul-friend meetings are like guideposts on the journey. The seeker may like to talk about something they want to give thanks for or some difficulty encountered.
- Pilgrimage and planned times set apart for prayer and reflection are an important part of the spiritual journey. The seeker may like guidance on what would be appropriate for their particular circumstances.
- As the soul friend and seeker explore the spiritual journey together, stories from the life of Jesus, the prophets, apostles and saints who have gone before give examples to follow and shine light into their own areas of

blindness. New insights help to realign their perceptions and priorities and set new goals.

- As their pilgrimage continues, their personal journey becomes more closely aligned with the holiness of Jesus and those who follow him.

- Regular time of prayer and meditation each day deepen their relationship with God. The soul friend and the seeker work out an appropriate plan together.

- The daily night prayer or review of the day (which St Ignatius of Loyola referred to as the *Examen*) helps to review experiences and events at the end of each day, develops a pattern of discerning God's presence in everyday life, and gives an opportunity to gain self-awareness and offer confession and thanksgiving.

Suggested reading

Ray Simpson, *The Celtic Prayer Book,* Volume One: *Prayer Rhythms – fourfold patterns for each day* (Kevin Mayhew, 2003), provides a pattern of daily prayer with a theme for each day of the week

Ray Simpson, *The Celtic Prayer Book,* Volume Two: *Saints of the Isles – a year of feasts* (Kevin Mayhew, 2003), celebrates the feast days of the saints throughout the year with stories about them. There are daily Bible readings for each day that illuminate our own personal journey and help to relate the lives of the saints to our everyday experience.

3. Rhythm of prayer, work and recreation

- The monastic way of life is based on the natural pattern of prayer, study, work and recreation. Rediscovering this in the midst of the pressures of everyday life is a challenge.
- The soul friend helps the seeker to discern their own life rhythm according to their personal gifts, stage of life and circumstances.
- This natural rhythm will include space set aside for personal prayer, corporate prayer, study, and rest and recreation for body, mind and spirit. It will also include family commitments, hospitality and paid or voluntary work.
- Over-busyness can be the result of needing to please others or due to insecurities leading to a need to take control.
- The practice of meditation may help the seeker to develop mindfulness and see more clearly the divine pattern for their life emerging.

Suggested reading

'How to make a Life Rhythm Plan' may be downloaded from the website www.aidanandhilda.org

4. Spiritual initiatives through intercession

- Intercessory prayer begins with listening to the desires on God's heart and praying until we see them fulfilled.
- The purpose of intercessory prayer is to overcome evil with good. This begins with our own inner

transformation that we may be more effective channels of God's grace.

- There are many stories about the effective intercession of God's people – for example, Moses, Elijah, Daniel and Paul. Making a study of these accounts gives many valuable insights on how to pray.
- God's story is our story and his dream becomes our dream. Helping the seeker to discern their deepest passions and concerns reveals the Holy Spirit at work and may indicate areas where God is calling the seeker to intercede.
- It may be helpful to make notes or lists for prayer and reflection.

Suggested reading

Joyce Huggett, *Listening to God* (Hodder & Stoughton, 2005).

Lance Lambert, *Watch and Pray* (Kingsway Communications, 1995).

5. Simple lifestyle

- Over time the soul friend will explore with the seeker how to apply simplicity in different areas of life – for example, home, relationships, church, work, money matters.
- The seeker may become aware of being too dependent on one or more of these areas to make life work. In the discernment process the soul friend may ask the seeker to describe areas of their life that give peace and those areas that create unease.

- All motivation leads towards a goal and determines our actions and habits. As trust grows in the soul-friend relationship, the seeker may want to talk about inner drives and compulsions that trouble them in relation to sex, money and need for control.
- Letting go of those things that we want to hold on to most brings freedom.

Suggested reading

Roger Forster, *Celebration of Discipline* (Hodder & Stoughton, 1980). The new edition of this classic Quaker text contains a study guide and covers how to live a deeper spiritual life following the ancient Christian principles of meditation, prayer, fasting, study, simplicity, submission, confession and worship.

6. Care of Creation

This may be approached in three ways:

Spiritual
The soul friend may invite the seeker to share how they experience God through the beauty, immensity, wildness and colour of creation, and describe their awareness of his provision through the seasons of the year. How does this inspire them to respond in worship, prayer and meditation, and how does it affect their desire to be a good steward of creation?

Practical
The soul friend may invite the seeker to share how they practise caring for the environment – for example, how they look after their house and garden and the local

neighbourhood, and how they shop and make choices about the use of their car and public transport.

Creative
The soul friend may encourage the seeker, as a co-creator with God, to develop ways of expressing their creativity – for example, in creative writing, art, music or gardening.

7. Healing fragmented people and communities

- Over time the soul friend may clarify with the seeker any areas in which they themselves feel to be in need of healing. This may include relationships with others.
- The soul friend and the seeker may also explore together the seeker's personal concerns for areas that need healing. This may be individuals, groups and communities such as their church, work place or the wider global community.
- The soul friend may suggest ways of praying for healing in these areas, how to mend a broken relationship, or how to mediate in a conflict. The soul friend may suggest people, resources or organisations that facilitate conflict resolution.
- In addition, the soul friend may suggest ways of prayer and pilgrimage to holy places to pray for the healing of the land. For those who are unable to travel an inner pilgrimage can be made.

Suggested reading

Russ Parker, *Healing Wounded History: Reconciling peoples and healing places* (Darton, Longman & Todd, 2001). Russ Parker is a leading teacher of pastoral care and healing in the UK and a member of the Community of Aidan and Hilda.

8. Openness to God's Spirit

> 'The wind blows wherever it pleases. You hear its sound, but you cannot tell where it comes from or where it is going. So it is with everyone born of the Spirit.' *John 3:8*

- Each of us tends to stifle the prompting of the Holy Spirit through ignorance, defensiveness, hardness of heart and fear of the unknown. The soul-friendship relationship helps these areas to come to the surface.
- There may be a comfort zone that God is nudging the seeker to become aware of, or a new horizon that might be opening up for them. On the other hand, the seeker might be a person who is always looking for new horizons and needs to establish stability instead.
- Finding the place of equilibrium where we are willing to respond to the leading of the Holy Spirit, whatever that might be, is one of the most important goals of the soul-friendship ministry. This place of inner freedom enables discernment and gives us the ability to make choices in line with the desire of God's heart.

Suggested reading

David Lonsdale, *Listening to the Music of the Spirit: The art of discernment* (Ave Maria Press, 1997). David Lonsdale is a Jesuit priest who has many years of experience in teaching the art of discernment and making choices.

9. Unity

The soul friend might approach this in four ways:

Personal
Does the seeker have an inner sense of peace, well-being and integration, or is there a strong sense of uneasiness?

Relational
Are there areas of conflict in relationships that need healing through forgiveness and reconciliation?

Spiritual
God is present is all things, and weaving the two strands of the spiritual journey and everyday life together enables the seeker to discover a deep inner sense of harmony.

Practical
There may be ways in which the seeker feels called to work towards unity by building bridges between church communities. Understanding and interaction with Christian denominations and faith communities other than one's own leads to unity.

In time the soul friend may introduce the seeker to the rich source of teaching and spirituality that is to be found in every church tradition and perhaps in other faith traditions.

Suggested reading

Margaret Hebblethwaite, *Finding God in All Things: Praying with St Ignatius* (Fount, 1987). Margaret explores prayer from the perspective that it leads us into deeper communion with God, ourselves and others and takes us on a journey towards discovering the presence of God in all things.

10. Mission

- When we pray, 'Your kingdom come; your will be done, in earth as it is in heaven', we are praying to align ourselves with the mission of Jesus. His mission was to reconcile the whole of creation to God and enable the earth to reflect God's glory.
- It is for us, then, to follow in the steps of Jesus and bring about the will of God, until the earth mirrors the beauty and the harmony of the Trinitarian relationship of Father, Son and Holy Spirit. As above, so below.
- Each one of us has a unique part to play. The role of the soul friend is to help the seeker discover their personal vocation. Only then can they find meaning and purpose and fulfil their part in the mission of Jesus.

  This vocation may be:

  – sharing faith with family friends and neighbours and work colleagues;
  – working for justice locally, nationally and internationally;
  – financial giving to the poor and those in need;
  – working towards healing and reconciliation in relationships;
  – caring for the sick and dying;
  intercession;
  – vocation for a leadership role in the church.

The soul friend listens to the concerns of the seeker and notices their gifting in order to enable the seeker to discern where God may be leading them.

Suggested reading

Ray Simpson, *Church of the Isles: The emerging Church in Britian and Ireland – a prophetic strategy for renewal* (Kevin Mayhew, 2003). Our personal vocation can only be fully realised when we discover our place in the Body of Christ and participate together in fulfilling his mission for the world. This book shows the vision of how the mission of the Church can be accomplished in the twenty-first century. Included is a twelve-session study guide.

Exercise

(For individual or group prayer and reflection)

Read through *A Pilgrim Way: New Celtic monasticism* for *everyday people* by Ray Simpson (Kevin Mayhew, 2003) and use it as a study guide for prayer and reflection.

CHAPTER 5

Coaches and whole-life disciplers

A further step up the escalator are those who coach or disciple others

A life coach might advise a client on:

- work
- home
- finances
- social life
- love
- dreams
- spirituality
- health

A whole-life discipler might also cover these areas, but whole-life discipling does not separate the spiritual from other aspects of our lives. A developing relationship with God is the foundation, and the teaching of the Bible and the experience of the Church are applied to each of these areas.

Whereas the term *discipling* is commonly used by evangelical Christians, the term *spiritual formation* is often used by catholic Christians. Whichever term is used, the aim is to be like those teachers whom Christ calls to 'prepare God's people for works of service, so that the Body of Christ may be built up until we all . . . become mature, attaining to the full measure of Christ's stature' (Ephesians 4:11-13).

Discipleship courses

The discipler and seeker may decide to work together

through a published spiritual formation or discipleship programme, such as those produced by Renovaré or the Navigators. Several such programmes are listed in Chapter 10.

These often lay the foundations of knowledge of Christ, the Bible or the Church, and these are, indeed, the right places to start, but few of them apply this knowledge to the whole of a seeker's life.

Spiritual fitness programmes

John Cassian (*c.* 360–435) was a Bethlehem monk who made extended visits, with his friend Germanus, to leading desert fathers. Later, as Bishop of Marseilles, he wrote two books about these visits which circulated in the British and Irish monastic churches. His presentation of fifth-century desert Christians known as 'Athletes of the Spirit', and the early 'Penitentials' of Britain and Ireland who were inspired by them, are forms of spiritual fitness programmes in which weaknesses can be viewed as hurdles that runners in a race have to overcome.

The principles are still valid today: learn to channel creatively energy that has previously been used in a negative way; instil a habit of appreciation, particularly of God's presence in all things. The way to achieve this is to go without comforts, to do good works, to practise constant praise and to start a healing process by making restitution to any wronged person.

Here are brief suggestions for a modern coach that relate to 'eight destructive passions'.

They are as follows:

1. Overcome gluttony with contentment

Gluttony may express itself in excessive consuming of food, drink, talk or internet. Over-consumption is frequently a compensation for lack of self-worth. A coach may suggest diet routines, but also meditation exercises that nurture a feeling of being loved by God.

Exercise

Lie or sit and 'sun bathe'. Visualise Christ as the Uncreated Sun, the Smile of God, pouring rays of love and warmth upon you. Visualise your body as a temple to be filled with these rays.

2. Overcome love of money with generosity

Avarice is love of money, which can lead to stealing, cheating, lying, manipulative business practices or workaholism that robs family and friends of one's presence. The antidote is to foster generosity in the seeker, which develops their trust in God's Providence and others' trust in them. A seeker who has cheated someone or stolen from them repays them, not from savings but from earnings or in service that costs something. The aim is to put ourselves in the shoes of the other person; it inculcates service as the model of supreme achievement.

Exercise

Give something each day – a donation, gift or helping hand – and savour the pleasure this gives.

3. Overcome rage with acceptance

This includes verbal abuse, violence to a person or their property, abortion. At the root of all these may be rage and unacknowledged pain. The aim is to become real about pain caused to or by the seeker which has been blocked out, and to make acts of restitution which brings a deep change of heart and self-acceptance.

Exercise

Visualise the person with whom you have been enraged, and relate to them with Christ's eyes, heart, words and actions.

4. Overcome self-pity with joy

Self-pity includes small-mindedness, resentment, complaining, indifference and despair.

How can we turn these reactions round?

Exercise

First, let your feeling of exclusion create empathy with millions of people who are excluded in worse ways than you are. Empathise with those who are excluded from any of the following:

a home
a decent diet
fair pay
a job
listening peers

Second, say thank you that God is here for you, that you are being welcomed into God's loving heart and purpose.

You can do this in any way that comes naturally. You can keep repeating the words 'thank you'. Others praise God in song or in what Christians call 'tongues'.

Third, thank God for this opportunity of being made one with the divine but human Christ in his rejection on the cross.

5. Overcome lust with love

In order to gain mastery over lustful cravings abstaining from sex was prescribed in early centuries. The seeker undertook not to live again in the same house with a person who had been a sexual partner, unless, of course, they got married. A coach encourages a seeker to develop close non-sexual friendships with people of both genders, and intimacy with God.

Exercise

Abstain from sexual intercourse, even with one's spouse (with their agreement), on, for example, Saturdays and Sundays, and offer your deepest parts and passions to God, until a deep communion infuses you.

6. Overcome slackness with attentiveness

Slackness includes neglect of duties, oversleeping, unreliability, wandering off without notice, lack of attentiveness to others, and slipshod work. In Celtic tradition, sleep was thought of as an image of death, and wakeful activity as a Christian's imitation of the Creator. So the aim is to motivate the seeker to a life of zeal, stability, perseverance and excellence, and in this way to become an icon of God.

Exercise

Upon waking, stretch your arms high, and pray, 'I dedicate all that I do today to you; I will do only what brings peace, and I will seek to do all things well and to rest, work and pray.

7. Overcome vanity with accountability

Vanity includes boasting and causing discord through promotion of ideas that are not God-centred. The coach helps the seeker to view themselves as a pilgrim and to develop trusting, child-like attitudes.

Exercise

The seeker pledges to their soul friend to keep silent during certain agreed forthcoming meetings, and give account to the soul friend at the next meeting.

8. Overcome pride with humility

Pride includes disregard of those in authority, envy, cheap criticism and contempt of others. The coach should excite a passion to be like Christ.

Exercise

The seeker names to the soul friend the person they most envy. They can meditate on Philippians 2:6-8 and then decide on a humble act of kindness they will do that person, even if it is anonymous.

Plan your own programme

Some soul friends and seekers may feel able to devise their

own programme tailored to the needs of the seeker. A discipler and a seeker may discuss which areas they wish to make a priority. Sometimes a seeker may have stopped growing, but does not know why. Perhaps the seeker has outgrown a form of devotion that was previously life-giving: a good discipler turns this apparent weakness into an opportunity to introduce the seeker to new approaches.

Here are brief notes on a few key areas:

Relationships

The soul friend will explore how well the seeker communicates at different levels with different kinds of people. The aim will be to move from passivity or aggression towards 'insightful confidence'.

They may talk through how to handle conflict. Things to avoid that make conflict worse are exaggeration, blame, bringing up unrelated issues, self-justification. The coach may suggest listening skills, and explore conflict resolution. This includes the ability to listen to the other without interruption, the acceptance of behaviour that the other has found unhelpful, clarifying behaviours both are willing to change; knowing when to 'park' a problem.

If loneliness is an issue, explore fear of rejection, and use exercises that enable the seeker to open up to love. If there are problems with love, explore whether these are rooted in fear of another seeing what the seeker is really like, fear of being rejected or taken over. Dealing with past hurts, developing respect, responsibility and care and learning to receive love are vital.

A booklet I have found most helpful, even though it includes only concise, clear course notes is *Relationships:*

Course Notes by Jennifer Minney (Silvertree Publishing, 2006; PO Box 2768, Yeovil, Somerset, UK.)

Work

A discipler may teach the theology of work, inspire a seeker to do each thing for the Lord, and to bless each colleague and customer. Then the frustrations need to be explored: strategies to deal with unacceptable work practices, difficult people, poor performance.

Time management

A *coach* may give tips on how to make the best use of time. For example:

- Have something to listen to or read when in the loo or a queue
- Deal with each necessary text, phone, mail or email message in the simplest, promptest way
- Create order in files and storage
- Keep a diary
- Combine routine tasks with pleasure viewing or listening
- Prioritise actions

A *whole-life discipler,* on the other hand, will explore the roots as well as the symptoms of poor time management. They will help the seeker see that God has given them authority and ability to evaluate demands made upon them, and will foster the seeker's confidence to refuse or postpone inappropriate demands when this is possible.

Exercise

Try the Activity Quadrant exercise.

Divide a blank sheet of paper into four squares. Write the following:

Important and urgent (in square 1)
Important but not urgent (in square 2)
Urgent but not important (in square 3)
Not urgent or important (in square 4)

In the light of eternity and your own calling, list the things you have to do that come under each category.

Now do what's in square one, plan what's in square two, delegate what's in square three, and bin what's in square four.

Talents and roles

A soul friend may ask a seeker to say what their talents are, and unearth dormant or unacknowledged gifts. One way to do this is to invite the seeker to express the dreams they have for themselves. Even if some of these are out of reach, they may provide pointers as to the direction the seeker might take.

Selwyn Hughes' *Discovering Your Place in the Body of Christ* (Marshall Pickering, 1982) is a classic manual that seeker and discipler can work through together.

Finally, a the soul friend and seeker could choose any items from the following list and add to them:

- a challenge to tackle
- a need to meet
- a person to love
- an injustice to right

- a skill to learn
- a discipline to master
- fitness to achieve
- knowledge to obtain
- a place to visit
- a fear to overcome.

CHAPTER 6

Co-discerners

Godly intuition

'I would like to live as a river flows, carried by the surprise of its own unfolding.' So the late John O'Donohue, author of many books on Celtic spirituality including the acclaimed *Anam Cara*, told a meeting. To accompany someone who seeks to live like this is a high privilege, and is far removed from the standardised packets of advice that may be appropriate at a less mature stage.

A further step up the escalator of soulfriendship are those who help seekers to discern their own unique calling. They not only teach, listen and pray; they intuit where a seeker is on the inside, and accompany the seeker in their own unique individuation process with God. In order to do this, the soul friend needs godly intuition and discernment.

The leader of a Café church told me that it consisted of new Christians who had completed courses such as Alpha. Each 'table' had a leader. These leaders knew their Bibles and how to lead an Alpha course. They knew how to prescribe, but not how to *accompany* an individual member of their 'table', starting at the point where they were on their inner journey. Could we help such leaders, he asked us, to get in touch with and use their intuition?

Many Christians who can teach or lead groups are ill-equipped to accompany new Christians on their faith journey because they lack awareness of intuition and how to use it; they need to learn to connect with people from the inside, not just the outside. How can a head-centred person develop their intuition with a view to emerging as a soul friend?

God has equipped everyone with intuition but few people recognise or use it as God intends, especially busy Westerners and Christians who think they know it all. Christ-honed intuition helps us to know the flow of energies and the spirit of a person, place or moment. It helps us to accompany another in a way that is attuned to their soul. Jesus' intuition grew until he could say, 'I only do what I see the Father doing' (John 5:19). That is our aim, too.

In this chapter we will explore how to develop three areas: intuition, listening and discernment.

Developing intuition

A dictionary describes intuition as 'an immediate apprehension by the mind without reasoning'. The Russian poet Pushkin describes it as 'the insights of the heart'. Nineteenth-century Scottish highlanders referred to it as 'keening', and many know it as 'the sixth sense'. A man who came to the Community of Aidan and Hilda at Lindisfarne for a job interview used the phrase 'holy hunches'. 'Although I like what you have here,' he told us, 'I sense no holy hunches.' He did not come.

Those of us who are more in touch with our 'left brain' may need to activate faculties associated with the 'right brain'. The psychologist Carl Jung gave new insights into the world of the unconscious. As Christians we believe that there is no area through which the Holy Spirit does not work and so we need not worry about taking Jung's advice to bore holes into the conscious mind to allow God to bubble up through our unconscious into our conscious mind and inform our present. Symbols, dreams and art are ways to do this.

The Bible overflows with stories of people whose intuition

was honed through experience. Abraham had an intuition that God wanted him to be willing to give him back that which he held most dear. In his case this was Isaac, his only son by his wife Sarah, a late gift after they feared Sarah was too old to conceive. His intuition did not mistake what God wanted, but it did mistake (no doubt conditioned by his pagan past) how God wanted him to express this. He ascended a mountain in order to offer Isaac as a sacrifice. At the last minute he saw a lamb caught in a tree. Then his intuition told him that God meant him to sacrifice the lamb, not his son. Perhaps he came to this insight by a combination of unease at killing Isaac and wonder at the 'coincidence' of finding the lamb. Centuries later Carl Jung would term this sequence 'synchronicity'. See Genesis 22:1-14; Carl Jung, *Synchronicity: An Acausal Connecting Principle* (Collected Works, Volume 8).

We may also develop intuition by being attentive to our feelings. For example, when we stay in a town for the first time we make for certain places or people. A chemistry draws us to them. These may be indicators of where God wants us to be. On the other hand, if we follow them as an animal follows a scent, with a mind for nothing else, we get attached to them. We are blind to the needs of others. Attractions then become attachments. Godly intuition is known by a sense of peace or rightness about such attractions.

Some suggestions for developing godly intuition

- Think of another Bible story in which the appearance of something unusual is intuited as a sign of God's leading. Relive this in your imagination.

- Look out for an example of synchronicity in your life each week. Keep notes.
- Paint or use clay to express what you are feeling. Then talk about what you have created with a friend.
- Look at something in creation – 'the Rock from which we are hewn' until it 'speaks' to you, for instance, flowers. Share or write down your thoughts.
- Get in touch with the four elements: fire, earth, water and air; become attentive to what feelings each evokes within you. Describe these in words or pictures.
- Become aware of the season of the year. What changes in light, temperature, sounds, sight do you notice? What do these 'say' to you? What feelings do they evoke in you?
- Become aware of the place where you are now. What is the spirit of this place? Think of a place that draws you to visit it. What is the spirit of that place? What are the elements that draw you? What do they say to you?
- What makes you happy? Write down your thoughts.

Developing listening skills

'You have ears, why don't you use them?'

Jesus (Luke 8:8)

'When someone is in a climate of listening they will say things they would not have said before.'

Dame Cicely Saunders,
a founder of the British Hospice movement

Listening is a key that opens doors to another person's growth. It is an art: with practice it can become a great art, but for many people it is a lost art.

A person should not become a soul friend unless they have first learned to listen; but many well-intentioned people are unaware that they fail to listen. Try out the exercise on listening to another person. If you are not perceived as being a good listener, take a course in listening before you try to be a soul friend.

We may learn to listen in various ways:

Listen to the body

> 'Your body is, in essence, a crowd of different members who work in harmony to make your belonging in the world possible . . . The inner voices of the body want to speak to us, to inform us of the truths beneath the fixed surface of our external lives.'
>
> *John O'Donohue*

Your body tells you, if you heed it, how your life is; whether you are living from a life-giving flow of water or from a poisoned well of negativity. Body language can tell us more than words. If a seeker avoids eye contact or has their head bowed, you know that their spirit is bowed down or bound. While the words flow, you will be asking yourself what they are really saying.

Listen to the feelings

The author, counsellor and psychotherapist Michael Jacobs likens this aspect of listening to 'trying to spot the bass line of a piece of music, while still concentrating upon the melody on the top line'.

Listen to the mindset

Every person is conditioned by the assumptions of those who shape them. This conditioning consists of a vast amount of information. Some, perhaps much, of this is misinformation. The soul friend will in particular look out for a mindset that stems from a false image of God, other people or self.

Many people project their experience of a parent on to God. So one person may perceive God as a distant Being who is not interested in the personal details of their life. A female who has been abused by men may perceive God as someone who wants to exploit her for purposes that are alien to her. Someone else may see God as cosmic energy, an expansion of their own (dysfunctional) life force. To break free from these false perceptions, and to know God as God truly is – total Love, Truth – requires the soul friend to identify and correct these misinformations.

A seeker may perceive the role of a father, a mother, a wife or a husband inappropriately. The soul friend needs to point this out in order that dysfunctional ways of relating may be faced, broken and made whole.

Listen to the past

In some situations a time of reflecting back is helpful, whether from recent experiences or from years before. This is especially suited to the vulnerable seeker who would shrink from answering questions that put them on the spot. For such a seeker, reflection can be a gentle meandering through past memories and related feelings that are recalled and owned and connected, and so become a healing influence.

Listen to yourself

Even the most experienced soul friend can become so overloaded that their own inner needs cry out to be listened to. These cries of one's inner child do not respect other people's boundaries. They have no manners. If this is your situation, it is vital to listen to them and to what they tell you about your own needs. If you find that the pressure of your own needs is impairing your ability to be attentive, you may ride it out, but plan prime time to deal with your own needs later. You may decide to reduce the number of seekers you see.

Sometimes a seeker reveals something of themselves which, consciously or unconsciously, triggers matters in your own life that have not been sorted out. Do not mix this with your soul friend's agenda. Talk it through with your own soul friend or supervisor. No two people's journeys are ever identical.

Listen to God

> 'I only say what the Father has instructed me to say.'
>
> *Jesus (John 8:28)*

When we listen to others we hear God's voice within them, but we also hear other voices – fear perhaps, self-pity, pride, domination or resentment. So the soul friend has to learn to distinguish God's voice within the seeker, within themselves and beyond both. Just as some people learn to speak three languages, so a soul friend learns to listen to three 'languages'.

We learn to listen to God through prayer, Scripture, conscience and our senses which can 'taste' goodness, wonder and love.

Through unease

Sometimes God can speak to us through a sense of unease. If you feel this as the seeker talks, you need to listen to yourself, because it may be that the seeker is journeying towards something that you yourself have not faced, so it is unease about yourself that is surfacing. Assuming, however, that you know yourself well enough to be able to discount that, there must be another reason for the unease. It may drift away, but if it continues, ask the Holy Spirit to bring its cause into the light and give it a name. It may prove to be any one of many things.

Let us take two examples. Perhaps much time has been spent working through bad ways in which the seeker has been treated, but then the penny drops that there is a spirit of rejection so deep-seated that everybody is viewed by the seeker with a jaundiced eye, whether or not they have mistreated the seeker. Now the focus must switch from the difficult people in the seeker's life to the spirit of rejection within the seeker.

Secondly, suppose a seeker has been frustrated that despite repeated attempts to find a creative and fulfilling job, they constantly end up in cul-de-sacs. You have worked on ways of moving out of those cul-de-sacs, but this does not seem to lead anywhere. The frustration seems endemic. You begin to feel uneasy. Then the penny drops. Seekers sometimes have such a low self-image that they unconsciously rule out doing any job which they really want to do. They assume that nothing they want to do could be God's will for them. The soul friend's task is to help them see that, once their heart is pure, their heart's desires may be pointers to what God has in mind for them.

Through givenness

At times God's voice comes as a gift. Perhaps this and that avenue have been explored, and the exploring has become a striving, driven by human adrenalin. Then a still, small voice whispers, 'You are looking in the wrong places. Accept my Presence in the situation you are in. You will know the place to rest in by the sense of givenness that accompanies it.' That is the cue for a change of focus. Become attentive to the course of least resistance.

Even some of the greatest Christian leaders have fallen into the trap of confusing their own ego with the will of God. A difference between the ego's will and God's will is that the ego tries to control others, whereas God tries to woo them. In the Cross, God is willing to 'lose' in order to win others. The ego imposes conditions, judges those who refuse to adhere to them. The fruit of the ego is judgementalism and tension. The fruit of the Cross is peace and love. A soul friend looks out for the spirit of control. Is the seeker open to being led in a direction that was not planned, that is not congenial, that requires others to increase in prominence and them to decrease; in other words, to sense the God-givenness in a situation and to embrace it?

Learning discernment

Discernment is the art of finding God's will in the concrete decisions which face us in life. It is the process by which we examine, in the light of our faith and our experience of God's love, what draws us away from God and what does not. Spiritual discernment is to distinguish what is authentic from that which is false. Discernment of good from evil is sometimes termed discernment of spirits. There is also discernment of God's will from among a range of good or neutral choices. And there is discernment of one's God-given personality and aptitudes.

As Christians interact with Scripture, church, circumstances, creation and inner conviction, they gradually discover what are the indicators of the divine will.

How can we learn to discern the Father's will as Jesus did? St Morgan, an esteemed fourth-century Celtic soul friend, offers some helpful guidelines. He went to Rome, where he was known by the Latin form of his name, Pelagius. He taught that God gave each person the ability to choose between good and evil, and that each had a responsibility to discern and follow right callings and conduct. He advises:

1. Learning God's general will for us from Christ's life and teaching

We must be honest with ourselves, recognising clearly those areas of our lives that we have not yielded to Christ.

Absolute honesty is an aspect of Light, which Scripture regards as an important test of what is in the will of God (see, for example, John 1:5; 1 John 3:24; 4:13). If we do not wish things about a projected step to come out into the light, it is probably not of God.

2. Weighing up good and bad consequences

At each moment of choice we must apply those principles in practice. To do this God has given us two vital tools. The first is reason: we can use reason to work out how God's spiritual law applies in each and every situation. Then we weigh up the good and bad consequences we anticipate are likely to result from each course of action. It helps to draw up two lists: on the first we write down what will be the likely consequences if we follow plan A; on the second list we note the likely consequences if we do not follow plan A. Then another two lists may be drawn up for plan B and so on.

3. Praying about our provisional intentions

We can be sure that, if we consider every choice carefully, and if we seek divine guidance, our decisions will please God.

The desire to do God's will is a pre-condition of finding it. A child-like attitude that brings everything out in the open before God makes discernment possible.

4. Sensing whether our actions bring peace or unease

If we have embarked on a course of action in good faith, but we find that the actions it entails do not bring us peace, then it is a sign that we need to go back to square one; we have not heard the Lord correctly.

Listen to what is deepest in our heart. Then write it out. If it does not accord with Christ, listen again. St Morgan believed that Christ frees us to become truly ourselves.

Four hindrances to discernment

We should not be surprised that discernment is a long, hard process, and that we can so easily get it wrong. St Morgan warns of four strategies of the devil which distort discernment. These can be presented in the following ways:

1. Giving up

We are tempted, and assume that we won't be able to keep to the path of God's will; we dread failure, so we 'stop the journey'. St Morgan calls this depression. He seems to recognise, as does modern medicine, that we may not be responsible for our depression; but he asserts that we are responsible for the way we respond to it.

In order to overcome this hurdle we have to be radical and cut through the web.

2. Haste

St Morgan regards speed as the great enemy of discernment. Much of our society is pressurised and driven. We may rush through life because we fear to face what lies under the surface. We rush to acquire or prove more than we are meant to. Thus we take short cuts and are economical with the truth. I tell a little white lie; in order to sustain this I have to tell another one, and another. I upset someone, or a group, because of an impatient or negligent approach. This causes criticism, and leads to more hurts, which breeds more misunderstandings. Then much more psychic energy has to be spent coping with the multiplying grievances. Little fleas have bigger fleas on their backs to bite them; bigger fleas have larger fleas, and so on *ad infinitum.*

Morgan urges us to take prime time to mull and slowly pray over decisions.

3. Complacency

When this sets in we no longer see people as they really are. We look out upon the world as if our ego is its centre, so we view everything with a distorting lens. The British call it the 'I'm all right, Jack' attitude. As far as we are concerned, the world can go by, so long as we get what we want. As the cost of loving escalates many of us grow weary and settle for much less than we had dreamed of.

Jesus had to use shock language to wrench people out of this distorted way of seeing: 'Before you can remove the speck that is in your brother's eye you need to remove the log that is in your own' (Matthew 7:4).

4. Indulging our cravings

Whenever we indulge our selfish cravings (St Morgan calls this instant gratification of desires), we avoid taking responsibility for something that we are meant to do or say. We put up defences within ourselves, and they become a barrier between us and others. When we live behind barricades, how can we discern what is beyond them? Jesus had to shock people out of this way of living by saying, 'Forgive your enemies.'

No two true duties conflict. But when we are trying to serve two masters, we fail to do right by either.

Finally, St Morgan points out that, even if we avoid the snares of the evil one, a decision made in good faith may still have bad consequences. The reason is that the web of life is complex. So we are not immune from things going wrong, even when we have made decisions with a pure conscience. We are responsible for making decisions in a pure conscience, we are not responsible for the outcomes.

St Ignatius Loyolas's insights into discernment

These ground rules for discernment have been built upon over the centuries. A Basque who lived in the fifteenth century, St Ignatius Loyola became almost a cult name for discernment and spiritual direction in the closing years of the second millennium.

Like St Morgan, St Ignatius said that each person has the ability to choose between good and evil. You don't question certain basic choices, he said, since they have already been made. If you are married, for example, you stick with your spouse through thick and thin, because God has already made clear in Scripture that that is his will. That still leaves you with many other choices. The next step is to be completely open to whatever the Lord desires for you. The third step is to say no to any choice that is evil – that is, which goes against the moral teachings of the Bible. The fourth step is to wait on God, ideally in a retreat, until God speaks with a voice so clear that you cannot mistake it. There is a time for a revelation from God, and it is possible to sense when this is. When there is no such special time of revelation, we should use prayerful imagination.

Again echoing St Morgan, St Ignatius suggests that we should use our reason to work out a right course. We should become tranquil, clarify the decision to be made, and look at it from the point of view of why we were created. Then we should weigh up the advantages and disadvantages of each option.

St Ignatius, like St Morgan, recognises that there is a deceiving spirit as well as a good spirit. Delusions and confusions can afflict us. Ignatius deals with this problem in his *Rules for the Discernment of Spirits* which he appends to his *Spiritual Exercises* (see Chapter 10). He came up with two indicators of the good or the bad way. Instead of using St Morgan's terms of guilt and peace, Ignatius uses the terms desolation and consolation. If our intended choices produce desolation, we should reconsider our choice. If they produce consolation, we should proceed.

St Ignatius advises us never to make a change during a time of desolation. Although desolation is from the devil, and can be brought on by our own slackness; sometimes God uses it to help us find a true understanding of ourselves, or to test us and so build our character. Our response to it should be to open ourselves like a defenceless flower before God.

Consolation, which comes from God, gives us a deep sense of being at peace in the will of God. The good spirit gives courage, strength, tears, inspiration. Anything that shakes our commitment will be from the devil; anything that builds our commitment will be from God. The danger in consolation is to coast along in our own strength or to become conceited. So Ignatius advises us to humble ourselves when we feel especially blessed with consolation.

St Ignatius concluded that a person who fundamentally wants God's way will feel desolation when they sin, or when the devil tempts them, and consolation when God's will is being done. The reverse, however, is true of a person who at heart does not want God's way. That person will feel apparent consolation or pleasure in wrongdoing, but desolation when influenced by the good spirit.

Although true consolation comes from God, the devil can mimic it in order to lead us away from our true path. How can we discern the difference between a true, God-given consolation and a false one? Pseudo-consolation can never give the deep peace and peaceableness towards others which is the fruit of God's Spirit. The devil can never fake unconditional love.

Exercises to develop discernment

1. Think of a choice you have to make. Draw up two lists of likely consequences if you do and if you do not follow

plan A. Repeat this for plan B. What do you think your choice will be?

2. Think about your fundamental choice. Are you clear you want God's will more than anything else?
3. Recall an experience where it was hard to know what you really felt. Can you put a name to your different feelings? What can you learn from this in the light of these guidelines?
4. Recall an experience of spiritual defeat. What dragged you down? What tactics did the evil spirit employ?
5. Recall an experience of victory that brought consolation. What choices or inspirations brought you closer to God?
6. Think of a choice you have to make. How would you advise another person who came to you for advice about the same choice?
7. Think of another choice you have to make. If you were on your deathbed, which choice would you wish you had made?

Further reading

Robert Van der Weyer, *The Letters of Pelagius, Celtic Soul Friend* (Arthur James, 1995).

Thomas H. Green, *Weeds Among the Wheat. Discernment: Where Prayer and Action Meet* (Ave Maria Press, 1994). This gives a concise outline of St Ignatius's advice on discernment, and each chapter ends with useful exercises.

Understanding types of personality

The psychologist Carl Jung and others discerned that psychic energy does not flow uniformly in all human beings. People manifest diverse spontaneous preferences in dealing with life. These do not predetermine people to a fated existence, but they affect the way we develop and interact with others.

The purpose of spiritual formation is that seekers become truly themselves, rather than copy other people. In recent years various methods that help us understand our personality have been developed.

Myers-Briggs Type Indicator

Myers and Briggs developed Jung's classification of personality types. Their courses point out that our dominant four characteristics are either introvert or extrovert, intuitive or sensing, feeling or thinking, judging or perceiving. This makes for 16 combinations. The value of finding out which of the 16 we are is that we can relax into our natural personality, and not be driven to be what we are not. A second benefit is in our relationships: we appreciate another person for their different personality instead of comparing them to ourselves.

A soul friend will realise that an introvert is renewed by solitude, unlike an extrovert who is renewed by social life, and try to enable that. A soul friend who is intuitive will cease to be irritated with a seeker for whom the outward senses are more important. An 'F' soul friend (Feeling Type) will accept that a person for whom facts and logic are primary will need to find a 'T' (Thinking Type) way of being God-centred. For example, they may ask questions such as what, when, where, how and why about a Gospel story. A 'P' (Perceiving) soul friend, who is at home with a hundred balls in the air, needs to know that a 'J' (Judging) person needs order and tidiness, and there is nothing wrong with that.

A healthy way to grow is to work on the aspect of our personality type which is weakest in us, and to practise understanding others' personalities. A soul friend may suggest ways a seeker can work at this.

The Enneagram of Personality

What is known as the Enneagram grew out of Sufi mysticism but was brought into Western understanding in the last century. It classifies people into nine types and explains why we behave the way we do. It offers pointers towards personal growth, and is a tool for improving relationships.

The dominant personality trait of each of us is one of the following: the Perfectionist, the Helper, the Achiever, the Romantic, the Observer, the Questioner, the Adventurer, the Asserter, the Peacemaker. The Enneagram system is taught by facilitators who help you to find your own personality type and will then offer you a safe space in which to explore your full potential.

If a soul friend versed in the Enneagram knows that their seeker is a Perfectionist, they will look out for hidden anger and explore ways to address the anger. They may encourage the Achiever to 'be', perhaps through meditation. They may encourage the Observer to do something practical in order to get a good life balance. They may encourage an Adventurer to stop rushing and stay with their feelings. And so on.

Yet another approach is to take the nine types of human gifts listed by the apostle Paul in Romans 12:6-8. Andy Raine describes these as 'motivations' in his book *Given for Life: Motivations* (see Chapter 10). Each person is invited to discern whether they are mostly a prophet, a server, a teacher, an encourager, a giver, a ruler or a mercy person. When I discovered that I was an encourager, I ceased to strive officiously to be an analytical expositor.

Working with dreams

Ira Progoff, the psychologist, says that, 'Recurring dreams are like persistent callers who have a message that needs to be heard.'

Some people feel comfortable about working with dreams and some don't.

Research suggests that most dreams are about the dreamer. There are a few exceptions, such as Joseph's dream about seven years of prosperity followed by seven years of famine (Genesis 41). But most of the dreams recorded in the Bible are about the dreamer. Ultimately, only the dreamer can know the meaning of the dream, but the soul friend can ask questions about the features of the dream, what the dreamer's feelings were, what resonates most deeply with the dreamer, and what the dreamer feels should be taken hold of. This has been called 'the tingle test'.

Carl Jung likens a dream to 'a little hidden door in the innermost and secret recesses of the soul'. He refers to a significant dream as an archetype. This synthesises for us our subconscious strivings for wholeness and gives shape to our instinctive hopes for the future.

Intuition, mental pictures, dreams and prophecies need to be weighed. Ask: which are from the ego and which from God? Which show wilfulness and which divine? The soul friend should keep the seeker focused on the feelings the dream evoked more than on the details.

Exercises

For a potential or actual soul friend

1. Find someone you can pair up with. Ask them to talk to you for two minutes about something that matters to them (it could be either a light or a heavy matter). Listen without speaking. After a few minutes echo back to them what they said, using their own words as much as possible. Then ask the other person to tell you what you omitted, wrongly assumed or got wrong, and how this affected their emotions. Discuss your emotions on receiving the other person's reflections on your listening.
2. Make a list of situations in which it is appropriate for a soul friend to initiate talk. Imagine a particular episode and what you would say.
3. Look back over the last 24 hours. What is the most significant thing God is trying to say to you?
4. Dream themes relating to stress include death, houses, missing the bus, going to work only partly clothed. Each person has their own stress dream symbols. What are yours?

Further reading

Anne Long, *Listening* (Darton, Longman & Todd, 1994).

Joyce Huggett, *Listening to God* (Hodder & Stoughton, 1995); *Listening to Others* (Hodder & Stoughton, 1996).

Exercises

Suppose you agree to be a soul friend, and the seeker arrives for the first session full of stress, bombarded with images and distorted by pressures which have been neither recognised nor addressed. It would be futile to begin by assuming the seeker is in touch with the deeps within. It is necessary to begin further back. Here are some possible steps that a soul friend might suggest in this situation:

1. Imagine there is a clothes line in front of you. What things on your mind can you, at least for the present, hand over and hang up on that clothes line?
2. Which of the stressful factors in your life do you think you can take in your stride without getting screwed up?
3. Arrange to make a retreat.
4. Build times of silence into your weekly schedule.
5. Consider ways in which you can learn to listen: to music, to your own body, to your spouse, or to creation.
6. Focus on yourself. Which of your reactions or convictions are driven or defensive? Which are positive convictions? If you are not sure, come back to these over a period of time. The hopes that will not go away may be the true convictions you should heed.

CHAPTER 7

Guides through the seasons of life

Not everybody who has developed discernment is called to stay alongside another through the various stages of life and through what Shakespeare's Hamlet called 'the slings and arrows of outrageous fortune'. Those who are so called may be thought of as one more step up on the escalator.

To the Celtic mind the sequences of creation's days and seasons are reflected in the human journey. Our lives should have dawns and twilights, springs and autumns, as well as sudden storms. A soul friend aims to be at home with these stages of the journey, has the privilege of accompanying another along part of their journey, and of helping them to make good transitions.

A soul friend becomes familiar with these seasons, and helps a seeker to journey through them with acceptance and confidence.

> 'We cannot live the afternoon of life according to the programme of life's morning.' *Carl Jung*

Let us look at some of these stages:

Birth

The author Philip Newell said:

> At the heart of life is the eternal womb, as Job says, from which the waters of life have burst forth . . .

> Do we see with inner sight that each plant, each creature, each human being is born at heart from holy soil?

Our nine-month journey in our mother's womb shapes the rest of our life. It is the place of well-being or non-being to which we instinctively return. In order to help a seeker, a soul friend needs to know their own birth, to embrace its pain and its wonder, to recognise God in it, to pray about it, and to see it as a springboard for the journey that is still unfolding. I made an imaginary journey through my own conception and birth following a most beautiful film of sperm, conception and birth. As Dr Frank Lake (author of *Clinical Theology*) described the different stages in the conception and birth process I, and others around me, relived our own changing emotions during this first journey of our lives. For some of us there was a period of bliss, such as Eternity intends for us; for others there was almost unbearable pain. For all there was a mixture of experiences. It is good to learn what we can from our mothers about our births, and to make our own imaginary birth journey. Then we can work at the process of acceptance of self, parents and God, which is affected in a significant way at birth. God uses 'post-operative prayers', so we can pray for the foetus, and for the transformation of distorted emotional patterns that may have begun at that time.

Adolescence

Adolescence is the period where possibilities and energies burst out and need a process of trial and error which can be checked out with an affirming adult. This stage has gone well if by the early 20s there has been sufficient separation from parents to create a sense of self, a work identity, a lifestyle and a set of values. A soul friend should expect turbulence and inconsistency. The primary aim should be to develop trust and good communication of emotions so that gradually the seeker becomes aware of the things that do not belong to them, of patterns that recur, and of eternal things of God.

Dr Frank Lake taught his Clinical Theology students to think of a four-legged wooden chair as an image of adolescent formation. A chair that is properly put together has the four legs of trust, autonomy, initiative, and industry; it has identity as its seat, and intimacy as its backrest. If it is not properly put together, the chair collapses when weight is put upon it. The role of a soul friend with a young seeker whose family facilitates these qualities is to enjoy interacting with the seeker's explorations. If a seeker has no such home background, the soul friend's role is to build these qualities both through their own relationship, and by exploring other relationships through which the seeker can develop these.

Weaning

Just as an infant has to be physically weaned from its mother's breasts if he or she is to move on in life, so, as adults, there are cords that need to be cut, and things from which we have to be weaned if we are to begin a new journey. For many, the developmental process is held back because they are inappropriately holding on.

A soul friend learns to sense when a seeker is still controlled by the opinions, values or violations of their parents, and is not free to make their own choices – for example, if an adult remains dependent upon a parent to the extent that they do not take responsibility for cooking, cleaning or budgeting; or if a spouse fails to give themselves fully in love because their primary emotional attachment is still to their mother or father.

Separation is the condition for finding one's true self. Sometimes this takes time. The soul friend may suggest small practice steps. Before a fledgling swimmer is willing to jump in at the deep end of a swimming pool, they may need to practise first wading, then jumping in from the shallow end. Gradually confidence builds up for the big jump.

In her novel *Mystical Paths* (HarperCollins, 1992), Susan Howatch describes how a son, Nicholas, whose mother's death devastated both him and his father, coped by believing that he was some sort of replica of his father. He tells his spiritual director, 'My fundamental problem is that I hate being me and I want to be someone else.' 'No,' the spiritual director informs him, 'your fundamental problem is that you hate being someone else and you want to be you.'

Nicholas' false self-image, which his father colluded with, led to one disaster after another before he was willing to face the reality. Once that time had come, the director asked father and son to face each other across a table, with himself seated between them at the end of the table. The time had come for 'the operation' when they would be separated psychically. The director prayed in the name of Father, Son and Holy Spirit that each would be aligned with the divine will. Then he asked them to grip each other's forearms, and he took a daffodil from a vase and placed it across their forearms. He asked them to reflect upon how confined they were by their present positions; their joined forearms deterred all spontaneous movement; how narrow and distorted their lives would be if they were always joined like that. For five minutes of silence they contemplated the full horror of that picture of the lives they had been leading. Then he asked them to relax their fingers, while still holding each other's arms, and to think about words from St John's Gospel:

> Whoever follows me shall have light . . . I have come that you may have life . . . Whoever believes in me, even though he was dead, shall live.
>
> *John 8:12; 10:10; 11:25, 26*

God's power broke through the false bond. Warm feelings towards his mother flooded into the son. Light shone. They both relaxed, moved back, and the daffodil, free now to be itself on the table, seemed to glow brilliantly. They began to live their true lives.

The three thirds of life

The physical phase

In the first third of life the body tends to be dominant. Energy expresses itself in physical activity, including sex, but also, for a sincere seeker, in mental dedication and in passion for God. Our journeying takes the form of putting a name to these and moulding them. That in turn requires us to work out our values and priorities. The seeker needs a vision of what fullness of body-mind-spirit means, and to develop clarity about boundaries and priorities.

Sometimes the natural release of energy that should come at this stage of life gets blocked or perverted. Then the soul friend has to help a seeker to identify and disown negativity. Once this has been done, creativity has to be released. That is a good time to explore longings and dreams. The soul friend may introduce the seeker to exercises which bring a balance between the physical and the spiritual, between the yin and the yang.

The mental phase

In the middle phase of life we become aware that there are, in Hamlet's words 'more things in heaven and earth . . . than are dreamed of' in youthful thinking. We become multi-dimensional, but, because the pressure to succeed is so strong, unacceptable tendencies, such as stifling ambition, lust, envy or rage, get pushed down, only to resurface, perhaps, in some form of midlife crisis. Then these emerge into consciousness and threaten the self-image we built up in early life. A soul friend can help us get to know this part of our being. During this mid-stage of life the soul friend encourages the seeker to learn, perhaps, about personality, gifts or danger points, and to develop good rhythms.

The spiritual phase

In the later years of life physical powers and restless activity tend to recede. The very fact of having survived the vicissitudes of life creates a certain security. There is space to become more aware of the spiritual side of life, and to contemplate eternal perspectives. A key question each person in the second half of life needs to face is this: 'Will I be responsible for cradling life in others or will I retire and live only for myself?' At this age we develop a need for both community and solitude.

The wisdom of old age is the wisdom of letting go. Sadly, many people who are old in years are not old in wisdom. The Venerable Bede relates how the elderly monk Egbert was stubbornly set upon going to Germany. He was operating as if he was in an earlier phase of life. The dreams of a brother whom he pressed to accompany him told Egbert to do a deeper work closer to home. In this brother's dreams, Boisil, the former Abbot of Melrose, directed Egbert to give input to the Iona Community, which, generations after Columba, 'was cutting a crooked furrow'. Egbert refused to heed these deeper voices, and set sail for Germany. A prevailing storm prevented them from sailing and capsized the boat. Only then did Egbert accept that he should work as befits the spiritual phase of his life. This story serves as a parable for us. We must go with the ebb as well as the flow of life.

When the journey comes to a halt

Life can come to a standstill in any of the three phases of life. The causes need to be looked for. For one person, the entrapment of dreary or demeaning duties can lead from weariness to resignation and bitterness. For another, the walk with God may be mixed with unacknowledged ambitions which have come to nothing. Without acknowledging it, they turn upon God and their spirit dries up. Or a keen pilgrim for God falls into a sin of passion and a barrier is erected between the pilgrim and God.

A soul friend helps the seeker to acknowledge what is happening. If a specific sin lies at the root of the impasse, it should be confessed and the assurance of Christ's forgiveness be given. If someone is simply tired out, the soul friend will explore with them how to have a break, a change, a stimulus or affirmation.

Autumn

The autumn of life is a time for harvesting the fruits of experience. You come to see ageing not as the dissolution of your body but as the harvest of your soul. In this way you achieve a new poise and belonging. Old age is a time of coming home to your deeper nature.

> One of the places where inner harvesting is most vital is the abandoned areas within your life. Areas of inner neglect and abandonment cry out to you . . . You can undo the damage that you did to yourself early on in your life.
>
> *John O'Donohue*

Retirement

A seeker has retired from employment and now feels redundant or swamped at home. A soul friend will explore with them the question 'What is life for?', and help them to grasp that relationship is the essence of life.

Retirement is the time when the seeker may be encouraged to think of the saints who were greeted and escorted to heaven. A soul friend will encourage a seeker to think about their 'place of resurrection'. That is, the physical place and the surroundings in which they wish to leave the physical body for the resurrection body, in the belief that this will have a distinctive influence upon those who remain in that place.

Dying

A soul friendship that deepens into old age can be a deep solace when one is dying.

The author Penelope Wilcock says about dying:

> To accompany another, along with their loved ones, up to the gate of death is to enter Holy Ground. To stand in an awesome place where the wind of the Spirit blows; to encounter peace and grief, insight, intimacy and pain on a level not found in ordinary living. By the side of the dying we learn stillness, waiting, simply being; the arts of quietness and keeping watch, prayer beyond words.
>
> *Spiritual Care of Dying and Bereaved People (SPCK, 1996)*

A member of staff at St Christopher's Hospice in London told me that three things stand out as most important to a dying person: relationship, rhythm and creation. A soul friend (even if it is a staff member who 'stands in' as a soul friend in a patient's last weeks) can encourage the dying person to talk about their nearest and dearest, what they want to say to them, when and how. Letters and messages might be conveyed through the soul friend to dear ones who cannot be present. The soul friend may draw out whether there are relatives or friends who need to be forgiven. Perhaps the dying person can voice their hurt or their forgiveness to the soul friend.

Rhythm means much – waking and sleeping, the light and dark of the day, and the rhythm of the seasons. The ongoingness of this life's rhythms reflects something of the other side, and brings reassurance and hope. Creation means much. A simple thing such as a ray of sun falling on a cheek becomes a cherished experience.

It is good for a soul friend to unfold memories for the one who is dying, to recall important events, to give assurance that there is nothing to fear. A dying person returns to the specialness of the moment, so it matters that we become present to the one who is dying, and become present to one's own grief only when away from the bedside.

By the side of a dying loved friend we feel helpless. But that very helplessness can be our best gift to the helpless friend. We can stay with them in peace, saying, 'I am here,' or stroking them in wordless prayer. From time to time, out of this silence, beautiful words of prayer may be spoken.

A soul friend may place a crucifix before the eyes of the frail or dying person. A well-known Bible passage, psalm or hymn may be read, and further prayers such as this may be repeated from time to time.

Sleep, O sleep in the calm of all calm.
Sleep, O sleep in the love of all loves.
Sleep, beloved in the lap of Christ.

May the angels tenderly bring you home
to the Three of limitless love.
Echoes a prayer from The Carmina Gadelica

May you be
as free as the wind,
as soft as sheep's wool,
as straight as an arrow;
and journey into the heart of God.

To be fully present when we come to that time of final parting, we need to have embraced death as a friend. It is said that St Columba took back to Iona a clod of earth from the grave of his friend, Ciaran of Clonmacnoise, and that he took this with him wherever he went. The present, however, goes to great lengths to deny the presence of death.

The Rule of Columba urged each member to prepare for their death. Saints Columba, Cuthbert, Brendan and others were given prophecies about the time and manner of their death; they died triumphantly.

A soul friend should prepare a seeker for death. That means learning to transfigure the faces of death that leer at us on our journey through life. One face is fear. Fear is rooted in the fear of death, of loss, of the unknown. Death, for a seeker who has been enabled to overcome fear, will be a meeting with a friend.

Fear flees as we become familiar with the company of heaven, and with the borderlands that form a bridge between earth and heaven. In the Celtic tradition the world of heaven was seen to be so close to the world of earth that death was thought of as an opportunity more than a threat.

The company of Celtic Christians on earth became friends with the company of heaven. They also sensed that the saints of God in heaven have a role in our spiritual formation on earth, as this prayer in *The Carmina Gadelica* reflects:

May God open to me every pass,
Christ open to me every narrow way.
Each soul of holy man and woman in heaven
be preparing for me my pathway.

A soul friend's prayers at the death bed

In the folk memory of the nineteenth-century Hebrideans, the Death-croon was chanted over the dying by the anam cara, the soul friend, assisted by three chanters. Later on the rite passed into the hands of the town elders and the mourning women who eventually sold their services as a profession.

Alexander Carmichael tells us in *The Carmina Gadelica* that prayers said by a soul friend over a dying person are known as death blessing. The soul friend makes the sign of the cross on the person's forehead, and asks the Three Persons of the Trinity and the saints in heaven to receive the departing soul.

Exercises

1. If possible, read an illustrated book or leaflet about the process of conception and birth, or look at a picture of an unborn child. Go on an imaginative journey of your own conception and birth. Write down your emotions and thoughts.

2. Draw a clock face without hands but fill in the numbers. Look at this and ask, 'What time is it in my life?' Wait until you feel the right time has suggested itself to you, and then fill in the two missing hands on the clock face to represent the time.

   If you are a soul friend with a seeker who seems unaware of their stage in life, look out for a timely moment to invite your seeker to do this exercise.

3. Draw in pencil a four-legged chair. Reflect on the development in yourself of the six attributes which make up the legs, seat and back (trust, autonomy, initiative and industry are the four legs, the back is intimacy and the seat is identity). Recall a quality you have which suggests you have gained something of each attribute and a keynote to denote the experience.

CHAPTER 8

Great soul friends

At the top of our soul friendship escalator (see page 9) are the great soul friends of the world.

Desert elders

The Christians who migrated to the Egyptian deserts in the fourth century knew that the soul, to know itself, must be able to pour out its thoughts to another.

Cassian, the fifth-century leader of the Marseilles faith community, who spent at least a year with the Christians in the Egyptian desert, learned the importance of a wise, holy, experienced elder who could act as a teacher and guide for another. Typically, such an elder would meditate deeply on Scripture and learn about the divine workings in the depths of human nature through his daily struggle against the eight destructive passions (see pages 44-48).

Cassian observed that the desert was pervaded by a deep spirit of friendship. He says of this indissoluble bond between friends, 'This, I say, is what is broken by no chances, what no interval of time or space can sever or destroy, and what even death itself cannot part.'

Transparency was the rule. Once a novice had come to trust an elder, he poured out all his thoughts – there was no point in hiding anything. The monks visited by John Climacus (*c.* 525–606) at Alexandria noted down every sinful thought which they showed to him. Climacus said 'If possible, sprinkle the feet of your judge and physician with your tears, like the feet of Christ.' *(Ladder of Divine Ascent, Steps 4, 56, 32, 39).*

The spiritual elder has great love, and does not bind his disciple. Abba Barsanuphius (died *c.* 540) writes to a disciple, 'I have not bound you, brother, nor have I given you a commandment, but an advice; so do as you wish.' Yet such was the love of certain elders that they would lay down their life for a disciple:

> The old man lifted the brother, and said to him, 'My son, put your hand on my neck.' The brother did so. Then the great man said, 'Very well, brother. Now let this sin be on my neck for as many years as it has been or will be active within you. But, from now on, ignore it.'
>
> John Climacus, *Ladder of Divine Ascent, Step 23*

Celtic soul friends

The author Edward Sellner, who writes about Celtic saints, says:

> Spiritual mentoring can be seen as a significant part of what historians have come to call the flowering of Ireland.

Early Irish and British Christianity drew deeply from the desert Christians for their understanding of soul friendship, and also from their pre-Christian experience of fostering young people as a supplement, not a substitute, to parenting.

The central importance of soul friendship is illustrated by the popular saying, attributed to St Brigid: 'A person without a soul friend is like a body without a head.'

Our main source of information comes from the lives of Celtic saints. Some of these were written up to two centuries after the death of their subject, and references to soul friends are often incidental; nevertheless we can glean from these some treasured insights. Here are a few stories.

Ita, foster mother of the saints of Ireland (*c.* 475-570)

Ita was born into an influential family. As a girl she dreamed that an angel gave her three stones and that these represented the Father, the Son and the Holy Spirit. The angel said to her, 'Always in your sleep and vigils the angels of God and holy visions will come to you, for you are a temple of God in body and soul.'

Before she could become a spiritual foster mother, Ita had to gain mastery of herself and of the spirits. She learned to fast and pray with great effect. Once she fasted for three days and three nights, during which time the devil waged war against her, and she resisted him. Eventually the devil left her with these words: 'Alas, Ita, you will free yourself from me, and many others too will be delivered.'

God directed Ita to live amongst the neighbouring people of Ui Conaill, where, with some companions, she established a convent. Young women flocked to her from all parts, as did the local people and their ruler. Ita prayed that God's Son might be given to her in the form of a baby she could nurse. She became known as the foster mother of the saints of Ireland. Her hermitage grew into a double monastery for women and men at the place now named after her, Killeedy, near Limerick.

Ita was one of those experienced and spiritually sensitive soul friends who could read people – even, on occasion, when they were not physically present. One of Ita's nuns, who lived far away in Ita's native Connacht, secretly committed adultery. Ita knew even this and requested that the nun be released to visit her. When Ita confronted the woman with what she had done it shocked her into repentance and she made restitution.

The infant Brendan was sent to her to be fostered. When Brendan asked her what three works were most pleasing and what were most displeasing to God, Ita replied, 'The three things that please God are true faith in God with a pure heart, a simple life with a grateful spirit, and a generosity inspired by love. The three things that most displease God are a mouth that hates people, a heart harboring resentments, and putting reliance upon wealth.' She affirmed Brendan in his desire to leave home and embark on an adventure, telling him, 'A foreign land is calling you so that you can instruct the souls of those over there.' It seems, however, that Brendan did not consult his soul friend over practical matters. When he returned from his first voyage, somewhat disillusioned with the setbacks they had suffered, Ita rebuked him for not consulting her about how to make the boats. 'He should have built them lighter,' she said.

Ita combined a lovableness with an awesome authority. Many came to her to confess their sins, even though they knew that she would not let them off lightly. They understood that she would require them to make restitution to a wronged person and so strengthen their ability to overcome weaknesses.

Ita did not give these penances, as they were called, for their own sake; she liked to build people up. A man once confessed to her that he had killed his brother. She sensed that he was truly sorry before God, so, to encourage him, she told him, 'If you carry out my counsel, you will have a happy death.' At some later date it was reported that this man had been killed in battle. When Ita heard this she told a friend, 'I promised that man he would have a happy end. Go to the place of devastation and call upon him in God's name and in my name to rise up. I believe he will come and meet you.' The man did just that, and lived long.

A story about Ita indicates the importance attached to a soul friend's role at death. When Comhganus knew that he was dying, he asked Ita to visit him and lay her hands on his lips and close his mouth at the moment of death. He felt God had revealed to him that a person on whom Ita laid hands at death would be borne straight to heaven. Ita thought this was not necessary. 'You will be glorious among God's saints,' she told him, 'what do you need from me?' Comhganus replied: 'Because of what I have asked no demon will dare to come near us on our journey, or to accuse us in any way.'

From *Life of St Ita* as edited by Charles Plummer in *Vitae Sanctorum Hiberniae* (Four Courts Press, 1910).

Maedoc (died 626)

Maedoc was trained at St David's Welsh school, returned to his native Ireland and founded communities at Ferns and elsewhere. It was claimed that Ireland's chief sage, Finn Mac Cumaill had prophesied:

> Ferns of the green strand!
> Excellent will be the man who will own it.
> Soul friends will come from here.
> It will be a place dear to God.
> Maedoc with his company will come
> Like the sheen of the sun after showers.

A company did indeed come there to Maedoc for spiritual direction, and many went on from there to be soul friends to others.

God gave Maedoc a most beautiful soul friendship with a monk named Molaise. Though Maedoc and Molaise loved each other deeply, they knew from the start that, as God led each of them onwards, it might mean separation. One day they sat praying at the foot of two trees that were to be axed. They asked Jesus, 'Is it your will that we should part or that we should remain together until we die?' One of the trees fell to the south and the other to the north. They took this as a sign that one of them must go south to found a new community, and the other north. Maedoc went south to Ferns and Molaise went north to Devenish.

At Ferns many people sought Maedoc's guidance. Among these were some Christians who wanted to know where their 'place of resurrection' would be. First of all Maedoc tried to discern whether, since these folk had been drawn to him at Ferns, that was to be their place of resurrection. So he asked them, 'Did any of you hear a bell ring when you arrived?' They did not. Maedoc wondered whether, though Ferns did not ring a bell, their place of resurrection would be somewhere within the region. He took them to a hill from which they could see the countryside around. They looked north, south, east and west, and Maedoc each time asked if the area before them rang a bell. None did, so he sent them on their way: they were to journey on until they found a place which did ring a bell.

Samthann, Abbess of Clonbroney (died 739)

Samthann was an astute prayer guide. A teacher, whose enthusiasm outweighed his wisdom, came to her and proposed to give up study in order to use the time to pray. The wise woman asked him a question: 'What, if it is not study, can prevent your mind from wandering all over the place as you pray?' The same man told her that he intended to go abroad on a pilgrimage. 'By all means travel overseas,' she advised him, 'if God cannot be found on this side of the sea. But since God is near to all those who call upon him, we have no need to cross the sea.'

A travelling peddler used to carry Samthann's greetings to the Friends of God (Celi De) in Munster. On one occasion she gave him this message: 'Ask Mael-Ruain whether he will accept my soul friendship.' When the young monk Mael-Ruain received this message he blushed deeply, bowed three times to the Trinity, remained in silence, and then said 'Yes'! When Samthann learned of his reply she is reported to have said, 'I think something will come of that youth.'

Ciaran (died 545)

The life of Ciaran of Clonmacnois portrays him as 'a soul friend . . . blazing with light and instruction'. Ciaran made friends throughout Ireland.

> When Ciaran was dying he waited alone in his little chapel for his soul friend Kevin of Glendalough to arrive. Unfortunately Ciaran died before Kevin arrived. However, Ciaran's spirit returned from heaven and re-entered his body so that he could commune with Kevin and welcome him. The two friends stayed together from the one watch to another, engaged in mutual conversation, and strengthened their friendship.

> Then Ciaran blessed Kevin, and Kevin blessed water and administered the Eucharist to Ciaran. Ciaran gave his bell to Kevin as a sign of their lasting unity.
>
> R. A. S. Macalister
> *The Latin and Irish Lives of Ciaran* (1921)

Findbarr (died 610)

When Findbarr was still a boy he was sent to live under the guidance of a soul friend named Lochan. A rich man named Fidach asked Lochan to be his soul friend. Instead of responding as Fidach expected, Lochan said to him, 'Kneel to that little lad there.' Fidach, insulted at the thought of kneeling to a boy,' stonewalled. 'If I take Findbarr to be my soul friend,' he parried, 'will you do the same?' To Fidach's surprise, Lochan said he would. Both men knelt before Findbarr and asked him to be their soul friend. The young Findbarr, with wisdom beyond his years, addressed his tutor: 'Will you please be responsible for soul-befriending Fidach and his offspring in return for teaching me the psalms?' The issue of how to pay for fostering seems to have been a mixture of good will and negotiation in due time. In this case, Findbarr seems to suggest that his act of giving back to Lochan the privilege of soul friending these well-able-to-pay people would be in lieu of his parents' fee to Lochan for teaching himself!

Another experience of Findbarr, also laced with humour, indicates that fees could be paid either in money or in spiritual kind. Findbarr had moved on in order to study the Gospel of Matthew and the Acts of the Apostles with Bishop Mac-Cuirb. In due course the bishop requested a stipend for his instruction. 'How much do you require?' Findbarr asked.

'That the resurrection of us both may be in the same place on the Day of Judgement,' the Bishop responded. 'You will have your wish,' answered the prophetic Findbarr, 'for you will be buried in the same place as I will be, and we will have our resurrection together.'

After another interval Findbarr went to live near Loch Iree. He started a school where his sister and many students came to live. In due course Findbarr himself moved on yet again to make cells by the lake at Gougane Barra, where fresh people devoted themselves to the Lord under his guidance. While he was there, Bishop MacCuirb died, and Findbarr himself no longer had a soul friend. He returned to Loch Iree and asked Eolang to be his soul friend. Eolang placed himself and his community under Findbarr's rule. Findbarr wept at this. 'This was not my thought; I intended to place everything, my soul and my community, under your guidance,' he sighed. 'Let it be, for this is the will of God,' replied Eolang. 'You are dear to God and you are greater than myself. I ask only one thing, that our resurrection will be in the same place.'

'That wish will be fulfilled,' Findbarr assured him, 'but I am still troubled about the soul friendship.' Eolang replied, 'You will receive today a friend worthy of yourself.' Eolang then took Findbarr's hand, and offered it to God, placing it, as it were, in the hand of the Lord. 'Lord, take this man to yourself,' he prayed, leading him to heaven. From that time, it was said, no one could look upon Findbarr's hand because of its radiance. So he always wore a glove.

The Celtic Britons

Soul friendship was also widely practised among the Celtic Britons and it was brought to the colonising English through Aidan's Irish mission from Lindisfarne. Bede wrote of Cuthbert, an English successor bishop to Aidan:

> Now Cuthbert had great numbers of people coming to him not just from Lindisfarne but even from the remote parts of Britain . . . They confessed their sins, confided in him about their temptations and laid open to him the common troubles of humanity they were labouring under - all in the hope of gaining consolation from so holy a man.
>
> Bede, *Life of Cuthbert*

Herbert was a hermit priest on an island in Derwentwater, who, Bede tells us, 'had long been bound to Cuthbert . . . by the bonds of spiritual friendship'. During Cuthbert's years at Lindisfarne and Farne Isle, Herbert walked across the land each year to spend time with him. After Cuthbert became chief pastor of the Northumbrians he made plans for a pastoral visit to Carlisle. Herbert decided to make Carlisle the venue for his annual visit. During their time together Cuthbert said, 'Remember to ask me now whatever you need to know and to discuss with me, for I am sure this is the last time we shall meet in this life, and that I shall soon move into the next life.' Herbert wept. On his knees he pleaded with Cuthbert, 'Remember your most faithful companion, and ask the Lord in his mercy that as we have served him together on earth, so we may journey together with him to heaven.' They never saw each other again. Herbert suffered a long illness. They both went to heaven on 20 March 687.

Soul friendship in the Western Church

Over the centuries the role of the soul friend was clericalised in the Roman Catholic Church and was neglected by the Reformers, but there were exceptions.

St Teresa of Avila (1515–1582)

There have been many spiritual guides and directors over the centuries from different lands and eras such as Teresa of Avila, who was a great spiritual director. Volume Two of her Collected Works includes her two books *The Way of Perfection* and *The Interior Castle.* These give bountiful advice on contemplative prayer, overcoming temptation and different ways of praying.

See *The Collected Works of St Teresa of Avila,* Volume Two, translated by Kieran Kavanaugh OCD and Otilio Rodriguez OCD (ICS Publications, 2002).

St Francis de Sales (1567–1622)

The letters of Francis de Sales, that busy Bishop of sixteenth-century Geneva, overflow with inspired spiritual guidance. Francis advocated an annual review with one's soul friend. The key question the director should ask is 'How is your heart – first, in relation to God; second, in relation to yourself; third, in relation to your neighbour?'

St Jean Marie Baptiste Vianney (1786–1859)

Jean Vianney, often known as the Curé of Ars, was the parish priest of a tiny rural backwater in nineteenth-century France. It was thought that his academic deficiencies would not harm the few simple, aged churchgoers. But he developed such discernment of spirits that he told people who queued to confess to him what their thoughts were, even when they were 20 miles away. His biographer, Henri Gheon, states:

> If the soul that laid itself bare before him was afraid, he gave it confidence. If it made pretences, he stripped it bare. If it gave only half its secret he opened it wide . . . That people might show themselves just as they were, he showed himself just as he was, in all his boundless love of God.
>
> Henri Gheon
>
> *The Secret of the Curé d'Ars* (Sheed and Ward, 1987)

The Celtic tradition today

What about the Celtic tradition of soul friendship today? Tom Cashman, a spiritual guide in the United States Order of St Aidan, writes, 'The Celtic tradition has the whiff of the perfume of the Mother, the Other Parent we have not known.' I believe it also helps to free us from one-sided, non-holistic ways of thinking and behaving, and re-connects us with our humanity, the earth and the Whole. The parts need to relate to the whole in a human body, in an organisation, and ultimately in all of life we need to relate to God as the Whole.

Soul friends in the Eastern Orthodox Church

The idea of the elder which arose in the Egyptian deserts has been retained in the Eastern Orthodox Church. The word for soul friend in the Greek Orthodox Church – *syncellus* – means 'one who shares a cell', an echo of its desert origins.

In Russia the word *staretz* is used. Bishop Kallistos Ware, the head of the Greek Orthodox Church in Britain wrote:

> . . . there is one thing more important than all possible books and ideas, and that is the example of an Orthodox *staretz*, before whom you can lay each of your thoughts and from whom you can hear, not a more or less valuable private opinion, but the judgement of the Holy Fathers.'
>
> *From his article on the Spiritual Father in Orthodox Christianity in* Cross Currents (Summer 1974)

The Russian Orthodox writer Fyodor Dostoyevsky (1821–1861) describes an elder such as he had met in Father Ambrose:

> An elder is one who takes your soul, your will, into his soul, and his will. When you choose an elder you renounce your own will and yield it to him in complete submission . . . to attain to perfect freedom, that is, from self; to escape the lot of those who have lived their whole life without finding their true selves in themselves.'
>
> *The Brothers Karamazov* (Penguin Classics, 2003).

Seraphim of Russia (1759–1833)

Seraphim lived as a hermit for many years. Later, Russians flocked to the cell of this, their greatest *staretz*, to receive even one word of life-changing guidance.

He often discerned the thoughts of a penitent even before they had reached his cell. When he was asked how this was so, he replied:

> I give only what God tells me to give. I believe the first word that comes to me to be inspired by the Holy Spirit and when I start speaking I honestly do

> not know what lies in the heart of the person who is questioning me. I only know that God directs my words for his benefit. But were I to give an answer out of my own judgement without having previously brought it to God, then I would make a mistake.
>
> Valentine Zander,
> *St Seraphim of Sarov*
> (St Vladimir's Seminary Press, 1975)

Such natural 'greats' – intuitives honed in the continual disciplines of prayer and reflection – are few and far between, and are not produced by courses in spiritual direction. But they inspire and beckon those of us who offer the crumbs we have.

Mentors of nations

At the very top of the escalator on page 9 are mentors of nations. Some of these are spiritual guides to leaders; others are shepherds, prophets, teachers to peoples, not just individuals.

In our global village our various peoples are adrift, aimless, hedonistic – an orphaned generation. That is the seedbed for disintegration and violence. Each country needs faithful carers who strive for the good of people in every walk of life. The Bible calls these people 'shepherds' – those who feed and protect their sheep. The prophet Isaiah glimpsed a time when national and local leaders would be like parents to their people, humbly honouring, serving, challenging and mentoring them as they waited on God (Isaiah 49:23).

In some countries monarchs once fulfilled the shepherd role. But who has taken this on from them? The State? The State does not love individuals. Politicians? They need the votes of selfish electors. Business and professional people? Even national services such as health and education are run as if they are businesses.

A true soul friend cannot be measured by money. People in love with money, power or celebrity cannot be shepherds. True soul friends of nations redeem charitable work and make it a nationwide engine of care, art and enterprise without strings. They defend all faiths and minority groups who seek the common good. Every land, and every level of society needs such people. In J. K. Rowling's *Harry Potter* books, Dementors are those who drag people down by feeding their inner demons. We need the opposite – mentors who:

- seek the best for each person without fear or favouritism
- come alongside and enable those who lack encouragement
- foster education, talent, creative art and science, and the things of the spirit

In ancient Israel such people, whether they were known as shepherds, foster parents or prophets, were not appointed but they were recognised. I believe God is calling into being such people in our lands today.

CHAPTER 9

Pitfalls and questions

Does the soul friend have to be free of faults?

Obviously not, but the soul friend does need to be orientated towards the light, to have purity of intention, and to be able to 'hear' a seeker's criticism. Only then can trust grow.

How does one terminate a soul friendship?

If it's dying a natural death

This may be because meetings have lapsed, or one of the two moves further away, or changed circumstances make it difficult to meet.

A simple card from the soul friend acknowledging that this has happened, thanking the seeker for what they have given is appropriate. The soul friend might use some such phrase as 'I guess this has run its course' or 'I realise this is not going to work in these changed circumstances'.

If the seeker is angry with a soul friend

If a seeker is angry with something the soul friend has said, it is important to meet and discuss this. A soul friend needs to challenge blind spots. Talk through what each feels. This gives the soul friend the opportunity to help the seeker face a challenge. If the soul friend feels the seeker is in denial and that no good can come from further meetings, the soul friend might suggest they cease to meet for the time being, but leave the door open in case the seeker has a change of heart later.

If the seeker is disappointed in the soul friend

If the seeker thinks the soul friend has failed to understand, stretch, challenge or advise them, it can be important that this is shared with the soul friend before making any decision. This gives the soul friend a chance to introduce into future sessions features that have been neglected. If that fails, then at the yearly review make clear you feel the time has come to move on.

If the soul friend feels they cannot continue

A soul friend may terminate the soul friendship for reasons such as these, which may be explained at one of the review sessions:

- I am now too busy.
- I have given what I have to give and I think you now need someone else to take you on the next leg of the journey.
- We do not seem compatible.
- I cannot give you what you want.
- I think there is a danger of dependency.
- I think you need a course of therapy for a while and then should come back to soul friendship.

It is important to make good endings: a prayer or blessing for one another in person or in writing, and thought as to who the seeker may talk to about finding a new soul friend. This can be helpful.

What about supervision of the soul friend?

The form this takes can vary to suit the people concerned,

who need to feel comfortable with it. Some soul friends go to an individual supervisor; others share issues with a fellow soul friend or in a soul friends' group meeting. Ways to do this are:

- Write a résumé of a session, or an extract of a conversation (names may be disguised).
- Reflect together on identifying expressed and unexpressed needs, responding to questions, ways of being attentive to the soul of the seeker and to the Holy Spirit, alternative strategies for overcoming problems.

What if the seeker is Orthodox?

The Orthodox tradition greatly values the role of the holy person, or elder, who is sought out as a soul friend. The seeker's priest should know about the soul friend, and formal confession of sins should only be made to the priest.

What about confession of sins?

Members of the Orthodox and Catholic churches are expected to confess their sins to a priest and some members of other churches choose to do this. Methods vary. One method is to prepare a written list of sins. Read these out to Christ with the priest as a witness. The priest offers a prayer, declares that the sins are forgiven, and may suggest a spiritual exercise or penance to strengthen the penitent.

A better way is for the penitent to say what comes from the depths of their heart. If tears come, that is good. A weight is offloaded. The penitent goes away freed and rejoicing.

It follows that if a seeker who is a member of these churches has a soul friend who is not a priest, the seeker makes confession in addition to the soul-friend sessions.

What about payment?

There is no rule – practices vary according to country and culture. In most countries soul friends charge a fee or invite a donation. In Britain, until recently, this was not the practice. Clergy who are paid a stipend that includes work such as spiritual direction, early retired people on a good pension and members of a religious community would not expect a fee. However, some earn their living in this way, as do many counsellors and life coaches. Others fall in between and welcome donations from those able to offer them. Some soul friends invite clients to contribute the equivalent of what they would earn in one hour.

A soul friend who requires a fee or who would welcome a contribution should explain this at the introductory session.

CHAPTER 10

Tools and resources

Questioning

Questioning is a tool a soul friend should use with restraint. Do not normally interrupt a seeker, but if the seeker moves on to a new subject before you have understood the previous subject, it is wise to ask a question for clarification. Sometimes a seeker is inhibited or confused, and then it can be helpful to ask a question that gently draws the deepest issues of the heart. Such questions can be blessings, helping the seeker to see more clearly for themselves.

Ritual

Ritual can be valuable and should not be underestimated, even if it is not part of the soul friend's or seeker's tradition. Forgiveness and release can be expressed through ritual acts such as washing, lighting a candle, holding a stone, burning written confessions, the use of scent or flower petals, anointing.

Candles, stones and crayons

Sometimes a seeker becomes locked in, and words dry up. Non-verbal forms of expression can unlock the heart and provide space for reflection.

A candle may be lit to mark a significant intention. Crayons can be used to paint a picture of something that words cannot express; or clay can be used to express deep feelings of anger or longing. Stones can be held in the hand

and can represent significant people, possibilities or problems in the seeker's life; then they can be arranged on a table or in a corner.

Parent-adult-child role play

Knowledge of tools used in counselling and therapy is too vast a subject to be covered in this book, but some of these tools particularly lend themselves to use in spiritual direction. For example, the Gestalt approach encourages a client to dialogue with three personae which they have within themselves: their immature self (child), their responsible self (adult) and their judgemental self (parent). A soul friend may discern when a seeker is being dominated by the first or the last persona, and point this out. A soul friend may invite the seeker to talk to or about this persona, then prayers of affirmation, penitence or release can be prayed for it. A soul friend might suggest that a seeker lays hands on their abdomen and blesses their unaffirmed inner child, or lay hands on their forehead and humour their inner parent which dominates other people. And so on.

The worst-case scenario

Suppose the seeker is so dominated by anxiety about a fraught situation that paralysis prevents sensible discussion or action. The soul friend might help the seeker look at the worst possible scenario, then at the whole picture, then at the possibilities. What if the worst happens? It is most unlikely that it will, but if the seeker can embrace and respond to this in imagination, the fear of the unknown is removed. The soul friend then gently leads the seeker to find their way around whatever the future may bring: 'Is God calling you to move out of or to assume responsibilities in this situation? If the latter, what boundaries for yourself should you decide upon?'

A journal

Keeping a journal helps some people to capture the lessons God is teaching them, rather like putting a snapshot in an album. Once a concern is on paper in front of them they can reflect upon it and come back to it. It helps them to monitor whether they are being truthful with themselves. It helps a soul friend to keep hold of the needs arising out of sessions with a seeker, and to blend these with the inspirations that are given them. Some seekers regularly bring their journal to a soul-friend session, and this can provide the content for the session. The value is that it enables the seeker to retain the most significant things that have impinged upon their life, and to offer these to the soul friend.

Information about referral agencies

Sooner or later it is likely that a seeker will need support from a source other than the soul friend. There are support agencies for almost every form of addiction, abuse, bereavement, trauma and disability, as well as developmental, financial or vocational need. A soul friend is wise to keep a list of such agencies to hand. Libraries or the local Citizens Advice Bureau often provide lists of local welfare, friendship, and counselling agencies.

Exercises for a soul friend

1. Prayerfully think about the condition of an actual or an imaginary seeker. Now let your mind range over the Scriptures. Which Scripture can you share with the seeker that speaks powerfully to their condition?
2. Choose an actual or imaginary seeker, and decide what type of personality they have (using either Myers Briggs, Enneagram or your own common-sense classification). Now think about which method of prayer you would recommend the seeker to try out, and explain this step by step.
3. Become aware of what your inner child is feeling. Talk to it and pray for it.
4. Discovering our shadow. Make a list of everything that is offensive to you in other people. Write in capital letters those things that are PARTICULARLY offensive. Then underline those particularly offensive characteristics that make you angry or that you feel are really despicable. You have probably drawn a fairly accurate picture of your shadow. Now walk or sit. Invite Jesus to come to the shadow. What does he do?
5. Begin to compile a list of referral agencies.

Resources

Courses

This is not a comprehensive list, and some courses available at the time of publication may not be repeated. Enquirers will need to make their own judgements as to their value.

Spiritual direction courses

The Retreat Association
The Central Hall
256 Bermondsey Street
London SE1 3UJ
Tel: 020 7357 7736
www.retreats.org.uk

Provides a list of training courses in the UK and some in Ireland. Some of these are also advertised in its annual journal *Retreats* listed under the programme of each retreat house.

Some Anglican and Catholic dioceses have occasional courses.

Some centres in the UK which offer courses include:

Allen Hall
(The Seminary of the Diocese of Westminster)
28 Beaufort Street
London
SW3 5AA
Tel: 020 7349 5600
www.allenhall.org.uk

Catholic Bible School
Nutbourne House
Farm Lane
Nutbourne
Chichester
West Sussex
PO18 8SD
Tel: 01243 371766
www.catholic-bible-school.org

St Antony's Priory (Ecumenical)
74 Claypath
Durham
DH1 1QT
Tel: 0191 384 3747
www.stantonyspriory.co.uk

The Missionaries of the Sacred Heart
The Croft
Bonvilston
Cardiff
CF5 6TS

A two-year part-time course in spiritual accompaniment.
Contact Tony Nolan
Email: tony_nolan@btinternet.com
Tel: 07914 955840

Ignatian Spirituality Centre (Ecumenical)
35 Scott Street
Glasgow
G3 6PE
Tel: 0141 354 0077
www.iscglasgow.co.uk

London Centre for Spirituality (Ecumenical two-year course)
The Church of St Edmund King & Martyr
Lombard Street
London
EC3V 9EA
Tel: 020 7623 6970
www.artsd.org.uk

Course Administrator: Mrs M. Wallace
St Mary Woolnoth Vestry
Lombard Street
London EC3V 9AN
Tel: 020 7621 1392
Email: ldcsd@spiritualitycentre.org

Abbey House, Glastonbury (Ecumenical)
www.spiritual-direction.co.uk
Contact: Sue Lloyd
36 Windrush Road
Keynsham
Bristol BS31 1QP
Tel: 01179 866503
Email: suelloyd@spiritual-direction.co.uk

St Margaret's Convent, Edinburgh
Contact: Elizabeth South
Tel: 0131 3461338
Email: ewsouth@yahoo.co.uk
Or: Alison Moody
Tel: 0131 229 4170
Email: malisonmoody@hotmail.com

Portsmouth Diocese
Contact: Mrs Kay Lancaster
Administrative Secretary
Mission & Discipleship Team
The Diocese of Portsmouth
First Floor, Peninsular House
Wharf Road
Portsmouth
PO2 8HB
Tel: 023 9289 9656
Email: kay.lancaster@portsmouth.anglican.org

SPIDIR (Spiritual Direction Network)
www.southwark.anglican.org/spidir/
SPIDIR organises regular training courses for those involved in direction ministry, as well as an annual one-day conference.

For East Midlands contact:
The Revd Lynda Randall
The Rectory
55 Church Street
Byfield
Daventry
NN11 6XN

For London contact:
Nicky Tredennick
Tel:01342 843570
Email: rev.nicky.hello@amserve.com
or Sally Fox
Tel: 020 8643 4407
Email: sklim2003@yahoo.co.uk

For Oxford contact:
The Revd Canon Barbara Doubtfire
Convenor of Spidir
6 Meadow Walk
Woodstock
Oxon
OX20 1NR
Tel: 01993 812095
Email: spidir@oxford.anglican.org

For Worcestershire contact:
The Revd Stephen Winter
The Old Palace
Deansway
Worcestershire
WR1 2JE
Tel: 01905 732813
Email: swinter@cofe-worcester.co.uk

For Yorkshire contact:
Sister Janet Elizabeth OHP
St Oswald's Pastoral Centre
Whitby
North Yorkshire
YO21 1RY
Tel: 01947 810496

or: The Revd Ann Coleman
Priest Director of Wydale Hall
York Diocesan Centre
Brompton by Sawdon
Scarborough
North Yorkshire
YO13 9DG
Tel: 01723 859270

St Beuno's Ignatian Spirituality Centre
St Asaph
Denbighshire
LL17 0AS
Tel: 01745 583444
www.buenos.com

Worth Abbey Centre for Spirituality
Contact: The Booking Secretary
The Open Cloister
Paddockhurst Road
Turner's Hill
Crawley
West Sussex
RH10 4SB
Tel: 01342 710318
Email: TOC@worthabbey.net

Other contacts for possible future courses:

Ely, Cambridgeshire
Contact: The Administrator
68 Pierce Lane
Fulbourne
Cambridge
CB21 5DL
Tel: 01223 575776
Email: jk27@cam.ac.uk

Leeds
Contact: John Sullivan
Lombard Cottage
Rawden
Leeds LS19 6RW

Leicestershire
Contact: The Ministry and Training Office
Church House
St Martin's East
Leicester
LE1 5FX
Tel: 0116 248 7000
Email: chouse@leicester.anglican.org

Loyola Hall Jesuit Spirituality Centre
Warrington Road
Rainhill
Prescot
L35 6NZ
Tel: 0151 426 4137
www.loyolahall.co.uk

Sarum College, Salisbury
Contact: Peter Tyler
Institute for Christian Spirituality
Sarum College
19 The Close
Salisbury
SP1 2EE
Tel: 01722 424801

Ushaw College, Durham
Contact: The Course Administrator
Ushaw College
Durham
DH7 9RH
Tel: 0191 373 8517
Email:courses@ushaw.ac.uk

International courses are advertised in *Listen: A Seeker's Resource for Spiritual Direction* published by the Spiritual Directors International www.sdiworld.org

USA examples include:

A master's degree in Soul Friending at The Lorian Center for Incarnational Spirituality
www.lorian.org

A two-year course in spiritual direction at the Haden Institute
www.hadeninstitute.com

Spiritual direction is taught at Mars Hill Seminary, Seattle.
www.marshillseminary.com

In Canada:

Providence Renewal Centre, Edmonton, Alberta; offers a two-year part-time course
www.providencerenewal.ca

In Australia:

The WellSpring Centre, Melbourne, offers courses
www.wellspringcentre.org.au

Pastoral psychology

Those who wish to explore the relationship between depth psychology and religion from the perspective of Carl Jung may find out about lectures and local groups from:

The Guild of Pastoral Psychology
13 Ascot Lodge
Greville Place
London
NW6 5JD
Tel: 020 3204 0175
www.guildofpastoralpsychology.org.uk

Ignatian spirituality

A number of Catholic centres run courses on Ignatian Spirituality. For example:

Loyola Hall (see page 117)

St Beuno's (see page 116)

Milltown Institute
Milltown Park
Sandford Road
Ranelagh
Dublin 6
Ireland
Tel: +353 (0) 1 2776300
www.milltown-institute.ie

Listening courses

Acorn Christian Trust sponsors Christian Listeners, a nationwide training programme in listening skills. Those who complete the training are used in listening ministries sponsored by churches and other groups.

Acorn Christian Trust
Whitehill Chase
High Street
Bordon
GU35 OAP
Tel: 01420 478121
www.acornchristian.org

Pastoral counselling courses

The Bridge Foundation offers training in Christian pastoral counselling using insights from psychiatry, theology and primal work.

The Bridge Foundation
12 Sydenham Road
Bristol
BS6 5SH
Tel: 0117 942 4510
www.bridgefoundation.org.uk

Life coaching/mentoring courses

Some people experienced in psychotherapy and spiritual direction are wary of this 'short cut' approach that may miss the deeper needs and meaning of a person's life, but there are at least two accreditation bodies:

The Association of Coaching
66 Church Road
London
W7 1LB
www.associationforcoaching.com

International Coach Federation
36 Freemantle Drive
Oakleas Estate
Wimblebury
Cannock
Staffordshire
WS12 2GZ
Tel: 01922 414980
www.coachfederation.co.uk

A search of the internet reveals many life-coaching courses. For example:

www.lifecoachingspecialists.co.uk
www.icoachacademy.com
www.ukopencollege.co.uk
www.schoolofcoachingmastery.com
www.coaching-life.co.uk

Mentoring

LifeServe offers a mentoring programme for Christians who are leaders in business or other areas.
www.lifeserveltd.com

Books

Soul friendship and spiritual direction

Joseph J. Allen, *Inner Way: Toward a rebirth of Eastern Christian spiritual direction*
(William B. Eerdmans Publishing Company, 1994)

William A. Barry and William J. Connolly, *The Practice of Spiritual Direction* (Collins, 1991)

William A. Barry, *Spiritual Direction and the Encounter with God* (Paulist Press, 1992)

David G. Benner, *Sacred Companions: The gift of spiritual friendship and direction* (InterVarsity Press, 2002)

Lavinia Byrne (ed), *Traditions of Spiritual Guidance* (Geoffrey Chapman, 1990)

Maureen Conroy, *Looking into the Well: Supervision of spiritual directors* (Loyola Press, 1995)

Kevin Culligan, *Spiritual Direction: Contemporary Readings* (Living Flame Press, 1983)

Tilden Edwards, *Spiritual Friend* (Paulist Press, 1980)

Kathleen Fischer, *Women at the Well: Feminist perspectives on spiritual direction* (Paulist Press, 1988)

Carolyn Gratton, *The Art of Spiritual Guidance* (Crossroad, 1995)

Margaret Guenther, *Holy Listening* (Darton, Longman and Todd, 1994)

Margaret Guenther, *Toward Holy Ground: Spiritual directions for the second half of Life* (Darton, Longman and Todd, 1996)

Tony Horsfall, *Mentoring for Spiritual Growth* (Bible Reading Fellowship, 2008)

Michael Ivens, *Understanding the Spiritual Exercises of Ignatius of Loyola* (Gracewing, 2000)

Gordon Jeff, *Spiritual Direction for Every Christian* (SPCK Publishing, 1987)

Morton Kelsey, *Companions on the Inner Way: The art of spiritual guidance* (Crossroad, 1984)

Kenneth Leech, *Soul Friend* (Darton, Longman and Todd, 1994)

Elizabeth Liebert, *Changing Life Patterns: Adult development in spiritual direction* (Paulist Press, 1992)

Anne Long, *Approaches to Spiritual Direction* (Grove, 1984)

Anne Long, *Reflective Practice for Spiritual Directors* (Grove, 2006)

Thomas Merton, *Spiritual Direction and Meditation* (Anthony Clarke, 1975)

Jerome M. Neunfelder and Mary C. Coelho (Eds.), *Writings on Spiritual Direction by Great Christian Masters* (Seabury Press, 1982)

Henri Nouwen (with Michael Christensen and Rebecca Laird), *Spiritual Direction: Wisdom for the long walk of faith* (HarperOne, 2006)

Susan Rakiczy (ed.), *Common Journey, Different Paths: Spiritual direction in cross-cultural perspective* (Orbis Books, 1992)

Janet K. Ruffing, *Spiritual Direction: Beyond the beginnings* (Paulist Press, 2000)

Martin Thornton, *Spiritual Direction* (SPCK Publishing, 1984)

John R. Yungblut, *The Gentle Art of Spiritual Guidance* (Element, 1991)

Classic letters of spiritual direction

Robin Baird-Smith (ed.), *Living Water: An anthology of letters of direction* (Fount, 1987)

John Chapman, *Spiritual Letters* (re-issued by Burns & Oates, 2003)

Derwas J. Chitty, *The Letters of St Antony the Great* (SLG Press, 1995)

St Francis de Sales (trans. Elizabeth Stopp), *Selected Letters* (Harper, 1960)

Robin Waterfield (trans.), *Streams of Grace: A selection from the letters of the Abbé de Tourville* (Fount, 1985)

Robert Van de Weyer, *The Letters of Pelagius: Celtic Soul Friend* (Arthur James, 1995)

Francis de Sales, *Introduction to the Devout Life* (Vintage Classics, 2002)

The Celtic tradition of soul friendship

Edwin M. Leidel, *Awakening Grassroots Spirituality: A Celtic guide for nurturing and maturing the soul* (Universe, 2004)

John O'Donohue, *Anam Cara: Spiritual wisdom from the Celtic world* (Bantam Press, 1997)

Edward C. Sellner, *Stories of the Celtic Soul Friends* (Paulist Press, 2004)

Edward C. Sellner, *Mentoring: The ministry of spiritual kinship* (Ave Maria Press, 1990)

Edward C. Sellner, *The Celtic Soul Friend* (Ave Maria Press, 2002)

The Desert tradition of soul friendship

John Cassian, *Conferences* (Cistercian Publications, 2005)

John Cassian, *The Institutes* (Newman Press, 2000). This includes methods of overcoming the eight destructive passions.

John Chryssaugis, *Soul Mending: The art of spiritual direction* (Holy Cross Orthodox Press, 2000)

Sister Benedict Ward, *The Desert Fathers: Sayings of the Early Christian Monks* (Penguin, 2003)

Discernment and listening

Ian Aveyard and David Muir, *Fit for the Purpose: The meaning of Christian vocation and how to respond when God calls* (St John's College Extension Studies, 1997)

Thomas H. Green, *Weeds Among the Wheat – Discernment: Where prayer and action meet* (Ave Maria Press, 2000)

Thomas N. Hart, *The Art of Christian Listening* (Paulist Press, 1980)

Joyce Huggett, *Listening to Others: Hearing their hearts* (Hodder & Stoughton, 1996)

Joyce Huggett, *Listening to God: Hearing his voice* (Hodder & Stoughton, 1995)

Anne Long, *Listening* (Darton, Longman and Todd, 1994)

Michael Mitton, *A Heart To Listen: Becoming a listening person in a noisy world* (Bible Reading Fellowship, 2004)

Russ Parker, *The Wild Spirit* (SPCK Publishing, 1996)

Coaching, discipling, mentoring and spiritual formation

Keith Anderson and Randy Reese, *Spiritual Mentoring* (Eagle, 1999)

Howard Baker, *Soul Keeping: Ancient paths of spiritual direction* (NavPress, 1998)

David Clutterbuck, *Everyone Needs a Mentor: Fostering talent in your organisation* (Institute of Personnel Management, 1990). Secular, but includes useful skills.

Emmaus: The Way of Faith (Church House Publishing, 2007). A three-year course.

Richard Forster, *Celebration of Discipline: The path to spiritual growth* (Hodder & Stoughton, 1980)

Bryn Hughes, *Discipling, Coaching, Mentoring: Discerning the hallmarks of Jesus' discipling* (Kingsway, 2003)

John Mallison, *Mentoring To Develop Disciples and Leaders* (Scripture Union, 1999)

Harold Miller, *Finding a Personal Rule of Life* (Grove, 1987)

Discipleship Journal – a bi-monthly publication. www.navpress.com

John Ortberg, *The Life You've Always Wanted* (Zondervan, 1997)

David Runcorn, *Spirituality Workbook*, (SPCK, 2006)

SEAN (Study by Extension for All Nations) www.licc.org.uk/imagine/resources/discipleship-courses/sean

James Bryan Smith with Lynda A. Graybeal, *A Spiritual Formation Workbook: Small-group resources for nurturing Christian growth* (Renovaré, 1999)

Keith Tondeur, *Escape from Debt: Christian Hope in Financial Chaos* (Credit Action/The Evangelical Alliance, 1993)

Dallas Willard, *The Spirit of the Disciplines: Understanding how God changes lives* (HarperCollins, 1988)

YWAM (Youth with a Mission) offer resources.
www.ywam.org

Companions for the Journey series published by SPCK (2004) includes:

Praying with Francis of Assisi
Praying with Ignatius Loyola
Praying with Teresa of Avila
Praying with Hildegaard of Bingen
Praying with Julian of Norwich

Personality types

Renee Baron and Elizabeth Wagele, *The Enneagram Made Easy: Discover the 9 types of people* (HarperCollins, 2004)

Isabel Myers, *Introduction to TYPE: A guide to understanding your results on the Myers-Briggs type indicator* (European English Edition) (Oxford Psychologists Press, 2000)

Adele Ahlberg Calhoun, *Spiritual Disciplines Handbook: Practices that transform us* (InterVarsity Press, 2005)

Malcolm Goldsmith and Martin Wharton, *Knowing Me, Knowing You: Exploring personality type and temperament* (SPCK Publishing, 1993)

Kathleen V. Hurley and Theodore E. Dobson, *My Best Self: Using the Enneagram to free the soul* (HarperOne, 1993)

Chester P. Michael and Marie C. Norrisey, *Prayer and Temperament: Different prayer forms for different personality types* (The Open Door, 1984)

Naomi L. Quenk, *In the Grip: Understanding type, stress and inferior function* (Oxford University Press, 2000)

Andy Raine, *Given for Life: Motivations* (Kevin Mayhew, 2007)

Suzanne Zuercher, *Enneagram Companions: Growing in relationships and spiritual direction* (Ave Maria Press, 1999)

Useful introductions to self-knowledge

Joan Hanger, *The Little Book of Dreams* (Penguin, 1998)

Thomas A. Harris, *I'm OK – You're OK* (Pan, 1976)

William Miller, *Why Do Christians Break Down?* (Augsberg, 1981)

Russ Parker, *Healing Dreams* (SPCK, 1987)

Russ Parker, *Praying with Dreams* (Cassette) (Eagle, 1992)

Allan Pease and Barbara Pease, *Why Men Don't Listen and Women Can't Read Maps* (Orion, 2001)

Claire Rayner, *Lifeguide: A commonsense approach to all your problems* (New English Library, 1980)

Philip Sheldrake, *Befriending Our Desires* (Darton, Longman and Todd, 1994)

Useful introductions to personal or sexual wholeness

Chester P. Michael, *A Call to Holiness and Wholeness* (a cassette learning course) (Open Door, 1992)

Leanne Payne, *The Healing Presence: Curing the soul through union with Christ* (Kingsway, 1995)

– *Restoring the Christian Soul: Overcoming barriers to completion in Christ through healing prayer* (Kingsway, 1996)

– *Crisis in Masculinity* (Kingsway, 1996)

– *The Broken Image: Restoring personal wholeness through healing prayer* (Kingsway, 1994)

Douglas J. Rumford, *SoulShaping: Taking care of your spiritual life* (Tyndale House, 1996). This includes questions for reflection and exercises.

Individuation and Jungian psychology

Inner City Books, Toronto, publish a series of books, some of which relate Jungian psychoanalysis to spirituality. For example:

Lawrence W. Jaffe, *Liberating the Heart: Spirituality and Jungian psychology* (1990)

Good and evil

T. T. Carter, *The Treasury of Devotion* (Longmans, 1960)

Russ Parker, *The Occult: Deliverance from Evil* (InterVarsity Press, 1989)

John Richards, *But Deliver Us from Evil: Demonic dimension in pastoral care* (Darton, Longman and Todd, 1978)

Sacramental confession

In the Catholic Church a booklet *Simple Penance* may be purchased from:

The Catholic Truth Society
40-46 Harleyford Road
London
SE11 5AY
www.cts-online.org.uk

In the Church of England a card for the traditional Confession and Absolution and a card for the modern Rite of Penance may be purchased from:

The Additional Curates Society
Gordon Browning House
8 Spitfire Road
Birmingham
B24 9PB
www.additionalcurates.co.uk

Two books which explore sacramental confession are:

Kenneth Ross, *Hearing Confessions* (SPCK, 1974)

Adrienne von Speyr, *Confession: The Encounter with Christ in Penance* (Nelson, 1964)

Guidance on Retreats and Pilgrimages

The annual magazine of the National Retreat Association lists retreat centres in the UK:
Retreat
The Central Hall
256 Bermondsey Street
London
SE1 3UJ
Tel: 020 7357 7736
www.retreats.org.uk

The Irish Missionary Union will send information on Irish retreat centres:

The Irish Missionary Union
St Paul's Retreat
Mount Argus
Lower Kimmage Road
Dublin 6W
Ireland
Tel: +353 (0)1 4923326
www.imu.ie

Pilgrim Adventure organise pilgrimages in Celtic lands:

Pilgrim Adventure
South Winds
Culver Park
Tenby
Pembrokeshire
SA70 7ED
Tel: 01834 844212
www.pilgrim-adventures.org.uk

Martin Robinson, *Sacred Places, Pilgrim Paths: An anthology of pilgrimage* (Marshall Pickering, 1997) contains guidance about the meaning and method of making pilgrimages.

Shirley Toulson, *Celtic Journeys in Scotland and the North of England* (Fount, 1995) outlines pilgrimages in Scotland and Northumbria.

Brian Brendan O'Malley, *A Pilgrim's Manual: St David's* (Paulinus Press, 1985)

Cassettes, CDs

Chester P. Michael *Spiritual Direction,* Volumes I and II (cassette/CD with book) (The Open Door, 1993). www.chestermichael.org

Russ Parker's book and cassettes on *Healing Dreams* and *Dream work: Techniques for discovering the creative power in dreams* (Paulist Press, 1983)